Little Wisdom

An Introduction To
The Way of Unity

Make me as stone
Flowing like water
In the Truth of my soul
In my True Nature
And moving always unto Unity
And Their image in me
The Unity Prayer - The Way of Unity

Land and Earth Acknowledgement

I am a global indigenous medicine man with a strong connection to Mother Earth. I am Sami by heritage and was raised in First Nations community, having been adopted into Six Nations as a child. I am raised in the teachings of both my Sami ancestry and the First Nations. I acknowledge the land and earth as my bones and body. I acknowledge the wind as my breath and the water as my blood. I am an extension of Mother Earth and acknowledge Her life as my own.

This work is written on the land of Tkaronto. I acknowledge the first peoples and indigenous traditions of the land this work has been written on. I acknowledge that I am a global indigenous settler on this land that has faced so much suffering. I acknowledge the ongoing genocide that the First Nations peoples face. To share the Knowledge offered here would not have been possible if not seeded by the wisdom of the First Nations. I acknowledge those who are keeping the fire lit. I acknowledge the daily struggle of surviving generational traumas and colonization. I hope this work can help to make people see what has happened, and is still happening, on Turtle Island. I acknowledge that the land of Tkaronto and all of Turtle island has been stolen from the First Nations, its original stewards.

I acknowledge the suffering indigenous nations have faced globally. I acknowledge the colonization of my Sami ancestry and the persecution of the Wiccan way. I acknowledge all the persecution indigenous people have faced globally, even those I do not know. This work, The Way of Unity, is an acknowledgement of the wisdom of indigenous traditions. Every word written in The Way of Unity is a word of praise to the wisdom of indigenous medicine traditions.

Recognition of Teachers and Teachings

As I write this work there are elders, teachers, ancestors, deities, guides, angels, spirits of nature, and other spirits from many ways of knowing who guide my words and add to this work. This work is also guided by Creator and Spirit-Who-Moves-In-All. It is my prayer and my devotion to write. I am saying, in this, that though I am the author I am not the only contributor.

As a practitioner I have been gifted the opportunity to learn from many ways of knowing, both in the physical world and the spiritual. To recognize the teachers and elders I have had I will add here sources for some of the teachings I have gained through my life.

I would also recognize my mother, who is a medicine woman, as my teacher. She has taught me much of what I know that has helped me walk this journey.

From First Nations Wisdom:
Medicine; The Inherent Power of Creation
The Medicine Wheel
Four Aspects of Being; Body, Mind, Spirit, Emotion
Sacred Silence
Plant Medicine
The Animal of Spirit, The Spirit of Balance
The Voice of Mother Earth
7 Generations
Honoring all my Relations
Equal Respect
The Power of Humility
The Seven Grandfather Teachings
Creator and Spirit-Who-Moves-In-All
All Things Are Borrowed
We Are Caretakers of The Earth
The Peaceful Warrior

Circle Teachings
The Voice of Spirit in All Things
Gratitude
Energetic Discernment
Intent
Observation
Word Medicine
Medicine Mind
Alignment with Natural Law

From Sami Wisdom, an Indigenous Peoples of Northern Scandinavia, Wisdom:

The Song of Creation
The Medicine of Altered States
Source
Harmonic Resonance
All We Are is Choice
Unconditional Love
The Soul Song
The Medicine Wheel
Four Aspects of Being; Body, Mind, Spirit, Emotion
Directed Self Awareness
Sacred Space
Keeping our Space
Sisu
We Are All Infinite
All is Vibration
Energetic Discernment
The Circle of Individual Space
Giving and Receiving
Journeying

From Wiccan Wisdom, an Indigenous Tradition of Northern Europe

The Divine Union
Magic is Prayer, Prayer is Magic
The Spirits of The Elements

The Search for Knowledge is Devotion
Purity of Heart is Fullness of Spirit
Speaking the Spirit of Creation
The Treasures of Heaven
The Nature of the Reception of Truth
Emptiness into Fullness; Absence into Presence
Seeking Truth in All Things

From Sufi (Islamic Mysticism) Wisdom:
The Naf/The Little Selves

From Egyptian/Kemetic Wisdom:
All is Mind/Consciousness
The Planes and Dimensions of Creation
Burdens and The Path of Eternal Life
Hermetic Principles
Body Magic, Stances and Movements
Word Magic, Words of Power

From Eastern Philosophy, The Tao Te Ching
The Way
Reflections of Nature
Energetic Movement (Qi)

This work is dedicated to:

All the medicine people of all ways of knowing who have given their life to Spirit's cause
And to all those persecuted for Spirit's Way

A medicine person refers to the person who would carry the wisdom, stories, and medicine of an indigenous nation. They were the healers and wise people of a nation. To me the Imam, the Yogi, the Buddha, etc... who keeps peace is also a medicine person. To me Spirit's cause is the fullness and Balance of all life.

This work is also dedicated to my mother and my sister, without whom I would not be alive today.

This is the beginning of a new journey.

"All is One"

"You Choose as You are Chosen"

"In the multiplicity of the finite, The Infinite is manifest"

Table of Contents

Practices and Prayers

"All things are made of equality"

"Truth is the path to sustenance"

"All things are created"

Universal Principle

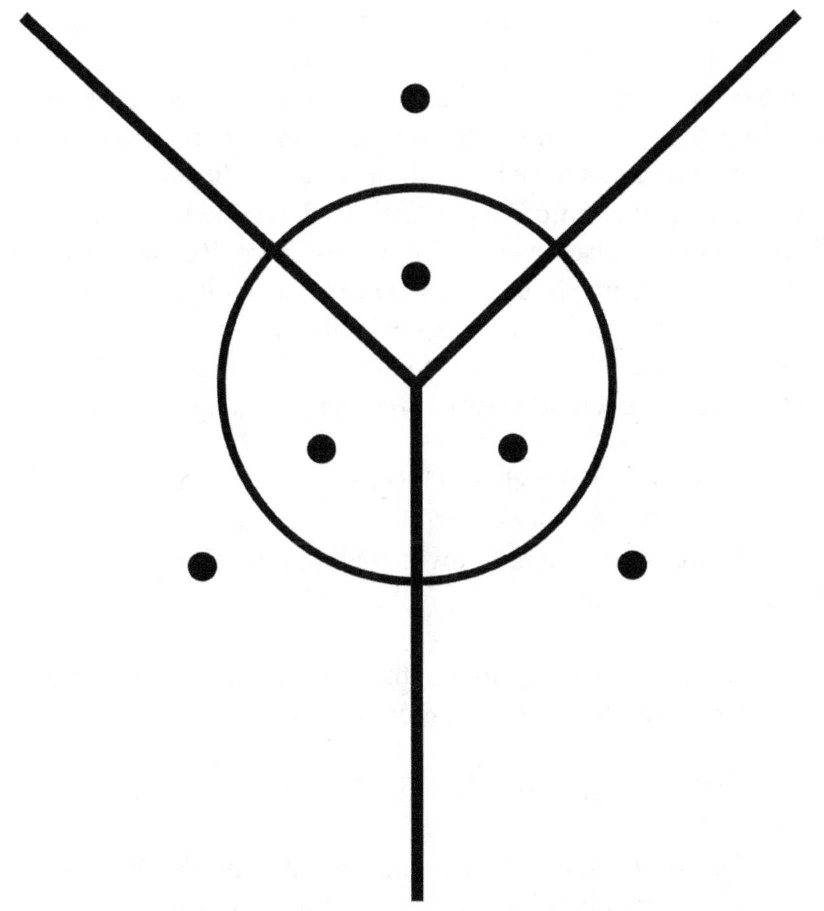

Universal Principles are the constant patterns that repeat throughout all of creation. Universal Principles are the Natural Laws that 'govern' all of existence. Through understanding Universal Principles and how they apply to us we may deepen our connection with the fullness of our life.

"All is One."

All of creation returns to Oneness in its most essential nature. Oneness is the origin of creation. The paradox of creation's existence is reconciled in the reality that all is conceived of Oneness. In physics it is known that all things must come from another. The Beginning must have kept all things within Themself to be. They are as a circle infolding at Their End, reconciling in Unity. Their End being, also, every point within Them, Beginning again. That 'Oneness from which all things came' is Unity. In every thing all things exist, yet also all things exist in their own Way to be. Creation is Creator's body. All is One is both a sacred spiritual teaching and an energetic law of creation akin to quantum physics.

Creation is the body of Creator

There is an inherent Power in all things. This inherent Power is called medicine.

'Right and wrong' are not thoughts in the mind of Creator. It is better to ask: 'does it sustain or destroy?'

GOD = Generation, Organization, Degeneration

The Way is the nameless and eternal Way. The Way is alignment with Natural Law. One who aligns themself with Natural Law walks along The Way.

The Way is also the individual Way. Everything is its own. It is for this reason that The Way is also the individual Way. Our individual Way is called Purpose.

"Within all things all Knowledge exists."

It is for the same reason that All is One that all Knowledge exists in all things. It is then that one must empty themself into True Knowledge. True Knowledge is to not know very, very well. When we come to the place of True Knowledge, which is to purely be, we gain a sight. That sight is the nature of genius. It is for the same reason that All is One that all knowledge exists in every thing. We must empty into fullness; absence leads into presence.

"We are all One"

All things are Oneness coming into existence. We are all our own Oneness. All things, also, are their own Oneness. In this we may perceive that the fullness of our own life is intertwined with the universal. The fullness of who we are is intertwined with the qualities of upholding all of life. This is the True Nature, the Self. The fullness of our own life is intertwined with the fullness of all life. We are all One.

"All things are created"

All things that exist are created. We must know well, then, that we may create fullness, for all things come from another. Within this Truth one may perceive the need of The Way, that it may be sought after by the steadfast. That all things are created means that all things which exist in this moment are made, not by the Spirit's will but by design. It is to design, then, that is the Spirit's will. To know the Spirit, then, is to know how to create. They are the Spirit of Creation. All things are created. We are creation manifesting and are our own creation manifesting. It is a dance, this building being built. To uphold Balance one must create Balance. The imbalances within the world are created, the way to peace will also be created.

In the wilderness of Spirit, Truth is a compass guiding us Home. This Truth is individual and universal, immediate and eternal. The Truth around and within us is a path to the universal Truths that govern creation.

"All things are made of equality"

All things are made of equality. The substance of existence is Oneness. It is for this reason that all things are made of equality. Within that essential equality it is by our place we are known. It is through upholding our place that we come to Know, for all things are made of equality. The one who finds it becomes free. We are not more, even, then a blade of grass except for the place we are given within creation. It is an Equal Respect.

We all have a True Nature. Our True Nature is who we are when we are in alignment with the energetic principles of creation. Our True Nature is, in this way, who we are in the fullness of our life. Our soul is the home of our individuality and is naturally interconnected with all things. Our True Nature is our clearest alignment with our soul. Our True Nature is who we are as our expression of our interconnection with all things. The True Nature needs no law to do good.

Our True Nature is integrative health. Who we are in the fullness of our life is a state of integrative health.

We all have a Self. Our Self is our pure sense of individuality. For those who are spiritually aware, they could perceive their Self within a light in the center of their head. Our Self is our True Nature.

Who we are in this moment is a 'house' our soul has built around itself to know the world. Our immediate being is an abode, a dwelling place, for our soul. Who we are, our 'self', is a building our soul has built. To turn this 'house' into a home for our soul is to realize our True Nature. When our life has become a home for our soul we will have become our Self.

"The Infinite is manifest in the multiplicity of the finite."

Creation is infinitely variable. Creation began with the potential of infinite variability. Difference is one of the great beauties of life. In the fullness of difference the Spirit of Creation finds fullness. When we cannot honor the Spirit of Creation for our differences, embracing equality, we become divided. This division is the loss of Unity. If difference was not a part of Creator's expression then creation would have never expanded. It would have remained a single super-condensed mass floating through No-Thing. At an essential, physical level difference is a defining trait of creation. All is One.

There is no discrimination in Heaven, in Unity. There is no dogma, no bias, no hate. In Heaven there is only Unity. It is division from 'Heaven' that is dogma, bias, oppression, hate, poison, etc... In Unity, which is Heaven, it is the ones who assume control, oppress, abuse, divide who are turned away and cannot attain. Not a thing is created except that it was created of Unity. Worldly discriminations are not thoughts in the mind of Creator. The Truth is not divided. Women and men are equally capable. Sexual orientation does not impact one's ability to attain. Heritage is a lens for divinity's Light, regardless of the land one's ancestry is from. It is the ones who are divided that cannot find True fullness. Truth is not ours to decide, it is ours to honor and respect. It is the thought of division that discriminates. It is the thought of Unity that knows peace. This peace is the gate to the treasures of 'Heaven'.

"You choose as you are chosen."

We are made to choose what is ours. Within us there is a soulful choice calling us towards what is ours. We are made for the things that are ours and are naturally called towards them. Our Purpose is made full through aligning with that soulful choice. We may grow distant from the clarity of our soulful choice. We are capable of becoming distant from our Purpose, for the soulful choice is made of Life. Who we are in this moment has always been guided by that soulful choice. Our True Nature is clarity of being. It is who we are as clear expressions of our soulful choice. We are made to choose what is ours.

"Choice is a face of Creator"

What a person is given to choose is a face of The-One-Who-Created-All within creation. All things move in this way. We are called by our life force to be as we are. That one may choose is a soulful expression, a Purpose, and within it, always, wisdom guides The Way. It is a journey of coming to a place of fullness of being in relation to life. When we can work with and honor the soulful choice within us we come to a place where we are walking the journey we have been given to walk. This Truth is universal, being that each is made of their own and all are made of Life. When we can honor the soulful choice of others, remembering it is made of Life, we step into the fullness of our own. Choice is a face of Creator.

"Truth is the path to sustenance"

Truth and Oneness are intertwined. The essence of creation is Oneness. All things are Truth manifesting. The one who aligns with Truth walks a path to the fullness of sustenance.

Fate's Paradox

Fate and free-will are intertwined. They harmonize within the essential energetic domains of creation as the soulful choice. This is Fate's Paradox. We have free-will and we are made to choose what is ours when we are full and healthy. It is because all of creation is Truth manifesting. As fate and free-will harmonize in the soulful choice they harmonize, also, in coincidence and manifestation. Coincidence and manifestation will operate in accordance with the nature of a person's soulful choice, their Purpose. Through understanding Fate's Paradox we may develop a clearer comprehension of the paradoxical relationships that are essential constructs of creation.

'Heaven', which is the state of Unity, exists in all things everywhere. Heaven is a state of being. The boundaries of Heaven are not life and death, rather the state of 'Heaven' is Life and all things renew in Death.

To attain Unity, which is the fullness of 'Heaven', one must reflect the nature of Creator within themself. A person must integrate deeply the understanding of universal principle until its upholding becomes second nature.

The great ways and traditions of humanity are as rivers running to the Ocean of Spirit. The water we drink from is still the Water.

The Way has no doctrine. It is not a tradition. It is an expression of the Spirit that exists within all things.

Enlightenment is not a great thing. It is a humble and Powerful thing. To place enlightenment, of any kind, upon a pedestal is to take away its Light. This does not mean one should not honor wisdom for its Way, it means that we must not deny enlightenment's attainment by placing it beyond our reach.

"We dressed The Way in the spirit of our people and it became our tradition."

Traditions are the way our ancestors honored and worked with Creator and the Spirit of Creation. It is the way our ancestors came to Know Life.

The greatest of goals is peace. In peace all other works come to fullness, without peace even success is empty.

"Neither give more nor take more than peace demands."

We each carry a True Nature that is our own. Within our True Nature peace is kept. The one who takes more than the peace of the True Nature needs will find themself emptied by what they've taken. It is also that the one who gives more than the peace of the True Nature needs will find themself emptied by their giving. It is to seek the peace of the True Nature and uphold the Balance that is neither giving more or taking more than peace demands that creates 'Heaven' in all people.

Life and Death are universal. They are not this life and the next. They are the fullness of life and the loss of life. The state of True life is Oneness. The loss of life is suffering. A person may choose death, and in that their soul does not know Life in this one and the next. A person may become Truly alive, entering into their Oneness, and in that they know Life in this one and the next. Life and Death are universal.

"1+1=Window, through which one may see the Truth."

Our unconscious mind is always processing information. When we can learn to align with the natural state of our mind, offering room for our unconscious to process information, the answers we seek come to us. Every thought we have is our unconscious showing our consciousness what exists within it. Our natural state is to align with this process within us. When we can align in this way a window opens. Through it we may perceive the Truth.

There is conceptual mathematics that occurs in all things. It is a 'quantum computation' based on the conceptual qualities of forces coming together to form a specified result. This mathematics is conceptual, the variable existing as its own entity. All things are energetic machines. To align with our unconscious is to perceive the underlying calculation of creation. A window opens that the Truth may be revealed.

The gate of The Way is always ready to be opened. It is not where we are or what we have done that decides whether this gate can be opened. It is our own will that decides whether this gate opens. This does not mean the path along The Way is easy. The one who lives in great imbalance will have to face much that the one who doesn't live in great imbalance will not. It remains that the gate of The Way is always present for the True and the steadfast who seek a better life.

"Within us all there is a well of Infinite willpower"

We are all expressions of the Infinite coming into finite form. We all have an infinite nature. It is our True Nature. Where we are aligned with our True Nature we are connected to our infinite willpower. When we are aligned with our True Nature we are connected with the part of us that can overcome all obstacles.

"What we do to the world around us is reflected upon our soul in equal measure."

The way we act within the world reflects upon us within our original essence, our soul. Soul is in all things. Soul is the heart of all things. Our own soul is interconnected with all things through Soul. Our soul is kept in the Oneness of creation. This is the reason we become burdened by cruelty and blessed by goodwill. The soul burdens or blesses itself in relation to our actions. When a person cuts another they also cut their own soul. When we hurt another, that same hurt is reflected as a burden upon our soul, our original essence. When we are compassionate in our way our soul reflects this. We feel a deeper sense of peace for that blessing. In this way what we do in the world is reflected upon our soul in equal measure.

"We experience the burden or blessing of our life's expression."

It is within the soul, the heart of hearts, that we are either burdened or blessed by our life journey. The burdened one cannot feel peace. They will always seek more and feel less for the sake of their soul burdening itself. We experience our burden or blessing. The one who upholds their relationship with the world, even that they are good to others for the sake of their own fullness, is blessed by their soul. They find peace even during difficult times. The burdened one lives in dis-ease in their heart; the blessed one Truly Lives and continues in their Way. It is a soulful reaction to our life's expression.

The internal manifests in the external; the external manifests in the internal. There is an universal energetic reflection that occurs throughout all of creation. It is a spiral of expansion and contraction. Through working with our inner-nature we will shape our external environment; through acting to improve our external environment we will transform our inner-nature. This is Natural Law.

There is a spiral pattern that occurs as all things contract and expand. As one becomes healthier they gain a greater clarity for how they feel regarding what they do, as they gain a greater clarity regarding how they feel they are then urged towards becoming healthier. As one begins to self-destruct they become unhealthy; as they become unhealthy they begin to self-destruct. This spiral pattern is a Natural Law that is present throughout all of creation.

Every action ripples out to the ends of creation and back again.

Spirit is a name we have given to the energetic realities of creation. Spirit is our experience of the energetic manifestation of creation. We perceived the Spirit as we gazed into the energetic worlds that exist beyond the material plane. We saw through our energetic interconnection the realities that exist beyond matter and came to call them visions of Spirit. Spirit is energy. Spirituality is living in alignment with the energetic nature of creation. Spiritual works are ways that we work with energy. Spiritual discipline is the action of discipline to honor and work with our energetic nature. Spirit is the name we have given to the energetic realities we experience. We perceived through our interconnection the Spirit of Creation, and They were sacred.

There is a greater movement in all things that is to purely be. To dance with and surrender to this greater movement is more powerful in The Way than struggling to reach where one perceives the goal. To 'struggle' for the 'goal' can become a way we reason to remain in suffering. We may say: 'I must always strive and never achieve'. To learn to be may be that we reach, yet that state has already achieved. To succeed is to surrender the reasoning that keeps us out of our fullness. It is to step into Life.

"A seed planted will bear its fruit."

What we bring into the world energetically expands upon itself, except that it meets opposition. When a person brings anger into the world the presence of anger expands both within the person and within the world around them. To harbor a belief of self-defeat will become a defeated life. As a 'seed' is kept it becomes the state of both our own life and the life of that which is around us. A seed planted will bear its fruit. It is for this reason that to tend our inner-nature, nurturing seeds of peace and abundance, leads to the fullness of all things. To sow a seed of discord is to reap a harvest of chaos. To sow a seed of dis-ease is to reap a harvest of illness. To sow a seed of peace is to reap an abundant harvest.

Purpose is not a thing driven to complete great tasks, rather Purpose is driven to finding its peace. Were a person to seek greatness without the sense of it bringing them peace they would lose their Way. To turn one's eyes to goals beyond peace is not the place of Purpose. It is to find one's place of rest that Purpose seeks.

"Life is One Work"

The Good Work, which is the True work of Spirit, is One Work. This Good Work is the work of bringing fullness into life for all people. Regardless of where we find our calling in this work, each one that takes part takes part in the One Work that is to heal the world. We all have our place in Balance.

There is a soulful alignment in creation that is kept within The Way. All things are urged naturally towards Balance. When we learn to listen to our unconscious and align with the universal Truths we step upon a natural current that is the return to Balance. This natural current, which is our True Nature's, is called alignment.

"As one grows closer to Unity the potential for individuality expands."

Within the cosmic equations that are the binding constructs of creation it is that as one progresses closer to Oneness the potential difference of individuality expands. It is for the same reason madness and genius are so closely related. As a person grows within their Way they expand as an individual, refining their sense of self. This creates a greater potential for difference.

All sciences, all ways of discerning thought, are the study of the anatomy of Creator. Their body is creation. All discerning thought seeks to understand creation be it theology, philosophy, biology, physics, or other sciences. In the beginning there was One, and from that One all was conceived. They expanded, weaving within Themself the energetic patterns that define creation. This was what we call the 'Big Bang'. It was Their outbreath. As one seeks to understand the workings of creation they are also seeking to understand the 'anatomy' of Creator, Knowledge is a face of Creator.

The application of Knowledge, being clear insight into the inherent Truth of creation, expresses two aspects. The first is wisdom, the fundamental aspect; The second is power, the expansive aspect. Knowledge, when applied, creates expansive opportunities in life, however without the wisdom of upkeep the power of Knowledge becomes destruction. As energy expands beyond its capacity for stability it begins to collapse, imploding within itself for expanding beyond its capacity. Without the fundamental wisdom expansion also becomes a reason for the collapse of a system. The Knowledge of physics, for instance, has given us many great opportunities, including the ability to destroy our world. Wisdom knows that Knowledge in the hands of the unwise is as bad as poison placed in the hands of a child.

All of creation manifests of No-Thing, however not a thing can Truly be nothing. Through attachment we lose connection to the substance of creation. It is No-Thing manifesting as All-Things. We do not lose our self by letting go. We gain our Self through letting go. Detachment connects us to the substance of our life when we can step into our True Nature. In absence there is presence; in emptiness one may be filled; in detachment one finds connection.

Through letting go we attain the fullness of Life. "If you love something let it go, if it returns it is yours." This is a Universal Principle.

It is more difficult to live in imbalance than it is to live in Balance. The one who destroys themself causes themself great pain, however to overcome this state of self-destruction they must let go of what hurts them. It is difficult to let go, to heal, however not letting go and returning to Balance is more difficult. "It takes more muscles to frown than to smile", and still so many people are caught perpetuating cycles of self-destruction.

Many of the great mysteries of creation are hidden within and behind simple Truths.

Those who see can never unsee, not because they would choose blindness but because they would never turn away.

Truth is the soil of 'Heaven'

Truth is a mountain around which we all are gathered. The many ways and traditions of humanity are faces of this mountain called Truth.

The human form is a way that the Spirit of Creation may walk in matter. Humanity is a meeting point between all realities, as all beings who walk the Spirit in matter are. This state of being is 'complex consciousness', to which is given Spirit, and continues, also, in realities beyond the material. Complex consciousness is the formation of the gift of co-creation. All beings who have a physical body and are gifted with 'complex consciousness', even beyond humanity, are meeting points between all realities. Were there 'alien' life forms they would also be our brothers and sisters for this reason.

Science and Spirit are inseparable

There is a Cosmic Evolution occurring of which humanity is a part. We are the potential of life reaching for its next step in the cosmic cycle. From Unity came the elements. From the elements, the plants came to exist. Creator urged within Themself and in creation, reaching for Their Light. After plants came the animals, moving in the world and experiencing Life. After the animals came the meeting point of Spirit and matter. Humanity is within the place of the meeting point. Within the meeting point complex consciousness begins to exist in matter. Beyond the physical planes of creation even more forms of life exist. These are the spirits, the demiurge, and the gods and goddesses. The Unity of Creator reaches into and through Life, Soul urging all things to return to Their Unity. We are part of a Cosmic Evolutionary cycle in which Life learns to walk in Unity.

Not one is denied the ability to attain except that their Purpose is upheld and Unity's principles are kept. There is not one among us who could not be as the greatest to have walked this earth. This is the Truth of Unity. In each and every thing all things exist. Not one is denied the fullness of Jeshua, nor the wisdom of the elders. Not one is denied the peace of the enlightened. All is One.

To bee or not to bee, that is the question.

The Primordial Elements

The Primordial Elements are the conception of the four Primordial Forces. They are: Mass, Interconnection and Potential, Force and First Power, and The Waveform; Earth, Air, Fire, and Water; Body, Mind, Spirit, and Emotion.

Earth/Body/Mass

As energy gains cohesion it forms Mass. Mass is the primordial element which later expands, in creation, becoming the principle of Earth. In our own life this principle is reflected as body. The expression of this primordial elements in the physical world is earth, or solids.

Air/Mind/Interconnection and Potential

There is a field which interconnects all forces. This field is also the potential for all forces to change their path of least resistance. Primordial Air is the interconnecting force that allows for infinite potential. In our life Air is thought and mind. Our thoughts are primordial wind passing through our unconscious. The expression of this primordial element in the physical world is wind, or gas.

Fire/Spirit/Force and First Power

All forces are urged to exist. This 'First Power', the urge by which all things come to exist, is Primordial Fire. It is the life-force that drives all things. Our energetic nature and individuality, our spirit, is the driving force of our life and is our own Fire. The expression of this primordial element in the physical world is fire, or sublimation.

Water/Emotion/The Waveform

There is a path of least resistance in all things. It is the waveform of the particle. This waveform is a field that bends both Time and Space as a force comes into existence. Within this waveform is the path of least resistance of a force. In our own life Primordial Water is Emotion, it is how we experience and react to the world. The expression of this primordial element in the physical world is water, or liquid.

The Path of Reconciliation

There is a path that is the path of returning to Balance. It is a universal energetic current existing in all things. This path is called here The Path of Reconciliation.

The Path of Reconciliation has three markers. They are: *The Healing Journey, Reconciliation,* and *The Universal Balance.*

The Healing Journey

Healing is universal. All things heal towards Balance. Even evolution is a healing work, for all things come from and return to Unity. Our healing journey is an integrative path of releasing suffering and stepping into the place of Balance that is ours to hold. That place is also the fullness of our life. When we walk our healing journey we help our unconscious release the things that keep us sick. We release the internal realities that keep us out of our True Nature. All things heal towards Balance. When we participate in our healing journey we release the realities that keep us out of Balance.

Regardless of where we are in life, our healing journey is valuable.A person who knows the things that heal them, their healing tools, is brought into the fullness of their life. A person who does not know how to heal, to release the suffering they hold, will always struggle with what they carry. In the healing journey we must develop the means to release our suffering and step into our fullness. These are our healing tools. Regardless of where we are in life our healing journey is valuable.

Reconciliation

Our heart of hearts, our soul, is as One with creation. In our most essential nature we are as One with creation. It is for this reason our soul may burden itself. We must earn the forgiveness of our soul in order to step into the fullness of our life. The soul becomes burdened or blessed by its action, and in relation to its True Nature. A person who has burdened their soul feels a weight upon them, and does not know Life in their heart. They must earn the forgiveness of this part of them. In reconciliation we take action to retrieve our soul's Truth and release the burdens we carry. We must reconcile for the suffering we have brought into this world for the seed of our Truth to find peace within us. It is because, as systems of coalescing energy, our most essential nature is as One with creation.

There is a great difference in quality of life between the one unburdened and the one who carries a great weight. It is within us all to release our heart of its bindings. The one who is burdened feels a dis-ease with life, and they do not know its True value. The one who is unburdened is joyful, for they have found the seed of True life and know well its value.

The burden will not respond to the healing journey. To work with burdens a person must reconcile.

The act of True reconciliation is an act of transformation. It is an acion of acknowledgement through which a person earns the forgiveness of their soul and learns to step into their True Nature.

There may be times we must reconcile for the ways of our ancestors. The burdens and blessings of our ancestors pass down in blood memory, and their burdens are held in place by a great Balance, expressing out from Oneness. A person may need to earn the forgiveness of the Soul of All for the actions of their ancestors to release their burdens.

The Universal Balance

All things in their most essential nature return to Oneness. We are all One. We are all the Oneness of creation manifesting in a singular, individual form. The fullness of our individuality is, for this reason, also the upholding of the qualities of the Oneness of creation. We are expressions of creation and so we are innately interconnected by the essential energetic laws of creation. We are all One because we are all Oneness manifesting. This is the universal Balance. It is equality, Truth, respect, etc… It is also justice, for Balance is The Way. The universal Balance is the fullness of Life, and the fullness of our own. The universal Balance is written in our own Way, for it is the fullness of our own. The essential nature of all things is Oneness. It is for this reason that the fullness of our life, where the True value of life exists, is within our own expression of Oneness. This is the True Nature.

The Path of Reconciliation must always lead to the universal Balance of Oneness. A person who persists in pursuit of Balance but does not seek to embody the spirit of Balance blocks themself. They place barriers between themself and their utmost goal. They place barriers between themself and the fullness of their life. The Path of Reconciliation must always lead to the universal Balance of Oneness.

The universal Balance is a work within the world. A person who works to bring the universal Balance into this world is mad full in their life. Their heart will bless them. They will know more joy and less anguish. It is because their soul is as One with creation that their heart blesses them for doing this good work. To work towards bringing the universal Balance into this world is a Powerful work that operates energetically to attract abundance.

When we honor our Healing Journey, our work of Reconciliation, and the universal Balance we operate in alignment with the energetic laws of creation. We step into Balance, and for this reason into the fullness of our life.

The Path of Reconciliation is the path of the enlightened. The enlightened all persist in pursuit of the universal Balance that is called here Unity. Enlightenment, however, is not a great thing. We are all our own expression of the Light. We all have our own wisdom. As a person persists in pursuit of Balance, walking their Path of Reconciliation, they grow closer to their Light. Those who have found enlightenment have all walked along The Path of Reconciliation. They have, in their own way, each, come to that place of Balance.

The Reconciliation is a work within the world. It is a work in which we bring the universal Balance into this world. The one who works within the world to bring in equality, for instance, walks the journey of the enlightened. They walk along the same energetic current of creation that the enlightened walk on. The one who works to reconcile for the actions of their ancestors walks a path towards the fullness of life. The one who steps into the universal Balance, even without specific action, steps into the fullness of life. The Path of Reconciliation is an energetic law of creation that means that the pursuit of True Balance will always lead to personal evolution.

The Sacred Heart

As our soul came into this world it left a piece of itself behind. That piece our soul left behind is our Sacred Heart. Our Sacred Heart is the part of our soul that never left Creator's Unity. It is the part of us that never left the Oneness of creation. It is, for this reason, that within our Sacred Heart exists the seed of our True Nature. We all have a Sacred Heart. Our Sacred Heart is the part of our being that never left Unity.

The Sacred Heart is aligned with universal principle. In its nature the Sacred Heart is kept in Oneness and so is bound by the principles of Oneness. A person who does not uphold Life universally cannot align with their Sacred Heart. A person who upholds Life universally naturally enters into alignment with their Sacred Heart. A person who aligns with their Sacred Heart becomes one who fluidly and naturally upholds Life universally. In this way the Sacred Heart is bound by universal principle.

Our Sacred Heart is the seed of our True Nature. It is the seed of who we are when we are most healthy and in alignment with Natural Law. One who seeks the fullness of their health aligns with their Sacred Heart, even without awareness of this energetic action. One who aligns with Natural Law aligns with their Sacred Heart, even without awareness of this energetic action. They become one who upholds Life universally and fluidly. One who aligns with their Sacred Heart, then, pursues the fullness of their heath and aligns with Natural Law.

There is no single expression of the Sacred Heart. The Sacred Heart proceeds throughout all tradition. To deepen our connection with our Sacred Heart is to deepen our connection with the part of us that is purely who we are.

To develop your connection with your Sacred Heart see: *Practices and Prayers - The Prayer of True Purity*

The Sacred Heart has five expressions. They are: *Innocence, Wisdom, Medicine, Purpose,* and *Original Design.*

Innocence

Our innocence is the character of our soulful directive. It is our innate individuality. It is the cadence of our soul song. Innocence is not child-like, however can take the image of our inner-child. It is, rather, the innate qualities of our individuality.

Our innocence is a song that expresses from our soul into our life. This song is our own and is a thing that has always guided our actions and choices. Our innocence is what decides whether we are called to medicine or to athletics. It is what decides our predisposition.

We are capable of growing distant from the clarity of our innocence. We are capable of losing our connection with our innocence. The innocence will often take the shape of our inner-child. When our inner-child is well within us our connection with our innocence is clear. When our inner-child is not well within us it is often a sign that we have lost connection with our innocence. Our innocence is the directive of our soul. It is not our direction. Our innocence guides us to what is ours and we must honor that calling. Within that calling we must also pursue Balance and fullness. In this way our innocence is a directive and not our direction.

The innocence cannot be bent or broken without losing the seed of the True Nature. A person whose innocence feels ill cannot bend their innocence into changing that directive, rather they must work with their innocence to heal and gain clarity. A person who does not work with their innocence, in the pursuit of a full life, will deny themself the energetic requirements of achieving that full life. Innocence cannot be bent or broken without losing the seed of the fullness of our life.

Our Sacred Heart holds the clarity of our innocence. One who aligns with the nature of their innocence naturally grows closer to their Sacred Heart. One who pursues alignment with their Sacred Heart naturally grows closer to the clarity of their innocence. That our innocence is innately interconnected with our Sacred Heart also means that our innocence is bound by the principles of Oneness. Our innocence may burden itself, and it is because it is a soulful expression. Our innocence, also, feels for the world, and in its own Way. Our Sacred Heart holds the clarity of our innocence, our innate individuality, and so that innate individuality is bound by the principles of Oneness.

Wisdom

We all have our own wisdom. Our wisdom is the way of thought of our True Nature. Our True Nature is the expression of our life that is aligned with our Sacred Heart. Our wisdom is, then, an expression of being aligned with our Sacred Heart. A person who is gifted to speak will have a wisdom that knows speech well. A person who is gifted to think will have a wisdom that knows thought well. Our wisdom is the thought of our True Nature. When we align with our Sacred Heart we move closer to our wisdom.

Medicine

We all have a gift to bring into this world. We all have medicine. Our medicine is the unique Power of our True Nature's expression. It is the unique gift of our way of being expressing. Within our Sacred Heart exists the seed of the fullness of our medicine.

When we grow closer to our Sacred Heart we hone how we express within the world. We become well directed and in alignment with our soul's nature. Through this we manifest the medicine that is ours to be. A person who is a speaker will likely find that their Sacred Heart holds the seed through which they uphold their gift of speech. Within aligning with their Sacred Heart they may find a deep meaning that gifts them the words they seek. In this way the speaker grows closer to their medicine. The one who is called to the warrior's way may find in aligning with their Sacred Heart the willpower they seek. A person who is an artist will find in their Sacred Heart the seed of the fullness of their creation. The Sacred Heart holds within it a map, and this map marks the fullness of our medicine.

Purpose

Our Sacred Heart marks our Purpose in this world. Our Purpose is made full in learning to be in alignment with our soulful choice. You choose as you are chosen. Our Sacred Heart holds our alignment with our Purpose. When we align with our Sacred Heart we step onto the journey of our Purpose.

Purpose is made full in being. Purpose is not always about a specific action. It is, rather, made full in learning to be as we are. Even before this life the Way of our True Nature is set down. We are given what is ours within ourself. What a person is called to is part of their Purpose. Who a person is called to be is their Purpose.

As our Sacred Heart holds the fullness of our Purpose, that Purpose must also abide the principles of Oneness. This means that Purpose comes from a place beyond greatness, for we are all All-Things manifesting. This means that our Purpose is deeply interconnected with our True Nature. It is deeply interconnected with who we are within the universal upholding of Life. This means that our Purpose is tied to our soulful health and that we are capable of growing distant from it.

Original Design

Our original design is a blueprint within our unconscious that marks our True Nature's expression in this immediate moment. It is a blueprint that marks our immediate fullness of being, existing within our unconscious. As our soul expresses into life it creates a defined 'structure' that marks our immediate fullness of being. This structure is who we are in the fullness of our alignment. This 'structure' then becomes a fundamental variable in how we work and operate. This structure is our original design. It is a blueprint that exists within our unconscious.

Our original design is our utmost potential. Our original design exists in alignment with our Sacred Heart and so our Sacred Heart is innately connected to our original design.

We are all already expressions of our original design. Our original design forms the fundamental variable of the algorithm through which our expression within this world is defined. The loss of the original design is an energetic 'distortion' that can take place within the unconscious. Beneath the surface of our immediate moment, in the essence and fullness of our moment, we are already our original design. In this way, to walk in alignment with our original design is to learn to purely be.

Our original design is a 'blueprint' kept within our Sacred Heart. When we align with our Sacred Heart we grow closer to this 'blueprint' that is our original design. To know our original design is a powerful way to create healing in our life. The one who orients themself on their original design, being also their alignment with their Sacred Heart, steps into the fullness of their life.

Eternal Law

In Eternity, Unity, there is a Law which, proceeding out, expands upon itself. Through these four 'Natural Laws' we may come to understand the Eternal Law by which all things are judged and weighed. All of creation is an expression of the Oneness from which all things came. In this way all things are bound to Balance. The Eternal Law is a cosmic equation that represents the relationship all things hold to that universal Balance. To explain the Eternal Law I offer four Natural Laws. Through them one may gain sight of the Infinite.

All Things Are Judged and Weighed

Every act, down to the smallest action, is judged and weighed. All things come from Oneness, the universal Balance, so there is a cosmic equation that weighs all things against Balance. Our soul is kept in Oneness. Our soul burdens or blesses us by our actions in this life. The one who acts in cruelty burdens their soul so they are burdened. The one who acts with wisdom blesses their soul so they are blessed. The one who acts in cruelty will find even the sweetest of deserts tastes bland. The one who acts with wisdom will find that even the most tasteless of things are filled with savor. All things are judged and weighed. All things come from Oneness so are bound to that universal Balance within the cosmic equation of The Eternal Law.

Evil is the Only Evil

Evil is to take from the fullness of Life. Evil is to live backwards. It is to choose death, destruction, division, etc... It is to create suffering. All things that are the destruction of Life are evil, for evil is the name we gave them. There is no evil but evil itself.

Evil is well measured by the creation of suffering, One who creates suffering has become evil. We must strive not to hurt others. In this relationship we must also remember that we are a part of Life. When we create suffering for ourself we have also become evil. One who creates suffering in the world, regardless of intent, has become evil.

Weight is Judged in Accordance with Context

The Eternal Law is a cosmic equation within which all things are held in relation to Balance. In this cosmic equation all things are measured. The 'weight' of all things that are judged forms in accordance with placement, context, intention, etc… It is not only the single action by which a thing is judged but all that has gone into its happening. The one who kills another to defend their family is not the same in the eyes of Creator, and of their soul, as the one who kills another in cruelty. In this we perceive that context, placement, intention, the fullness of the moment, exist in every 'judgment'. The 'judgment' of that cosmic equation is made within the full context of an occurrence.

There is No Exception

There is no exception in the Eternal Law. All things are judged and weighed in accordance with this cosmic equation. Creator does not care if a person is a king or a beggar. They will be equal within Their Balance. There is no exception to Balance. The moment there would become an exception is the moment the Balance would be lost. There can be no exception in Them.

The Temple

She reaches the top of the small staircase. Looking up she sees doors of old wood, worn by the ages. The building is small and unadorned, hidden in the center of a mountain valley. Old growth vines cover its walls, flowers blooming from them with a vibrancy she has never seen before. The sun sets over a mountain's peak as she stands in front of the doors. She turns to look back towards where she came from. The sky is painted orange and purple, coloring the moment in a serene light. Her world falls into a deepening Silence.

She can feel a life within the building that is its own. Touching the door, she feels a heartbeat pulsing against her hand. It comes from within The Temple.

She has been seeking this place for many years.

She stops in front of the doors, remembering what her elder had shared with her. *"It is hidden away at the center of all things, Silent and waiting. Find it, my child, and you will have found the source of everything you seek in this world."* The voice echoes in her mind.

She reaches for the doors again. Her touch sparks a thought. She wonders for the first time in a long while if she really wants to know. She wonders if she is ready for what lives within. Taking a deep breath she opens the door.

Standing at its threshold, she looks within. She sees only darkness within. It is a darkness vast as the night sky. As she looks closer, her eyes straining, she sees a small light shining in the far distance. A warmth rises within her heart at its sight. She yearns to Know.

"Follow your heart" echoes the voice of her elder in her mind.

She steps past the threshold. The door closes behind her, thudding shut and enveloping her in darkness.

Her mind begins to whirl and spin. Everything loses focus. She forgets herself and cannot remember the light. The darkness all around her closes in, suffocating her. She feels so alone. She drops to her knees, clutching her head in both hands and weeps. A panic rises within her as the spinning grows more and more intense. The tears become a flood. The light in the distance fades, swallowed by the darkness. All that is left is the abyss within The Temple.

She weeps, feeling the darkness' cold embrace on her skin. She cries out, her pain expanding through the space out to the ends of creation.

A vision of her elder appears in front of her. Her elder takes form in the dark, a vision of light. There is a warmth emanating from the light of her elder. In the cold emptiness of this space it is a reminder of hope. Her elder places a hand on her shoulder. A comforting warmth spreads through her body, chasing away the shadow's hands and releasing the hold the darkness has on her. She calms down, remembering herself.

She looks up to see one she'd lost long ago. She lowers her head again and weeps briefly.

Her elder waits patiently, holding love.

"The way leads through darkness." speaks the spirit of her elder. *"You always knew this."* There is a small laugh underneath her elder's words. *"Why have you fallen when this is the journey you chose?"* There is a smile on the elder's face that acknowledges her struggle with unconditional love. It is a playful smile that reminds her of when she was younger. She remembers the games her elder used to play with her. She remembers them fondly and laughs through her tears at how they'd frustrate her.

"What do I do?!" She asks, despair filling her voice.

"You carry on or you leave." The spirit of her elder speaks. The small light appears in the distance of The Temple and the door opens behind her, revealing the valley she had just left. It feels like she has been in this place for hours yet the last rays of light still shine upon the mountain valley.

Her elder's spirit fades. As the hand leaves her shoulder she feels the cold return. There is a warmth that has risen from within her that keeps the despair at bay. She feels less for her elder's passage and more for her elder's presence.

"After this there is no turning back." Echoes her elder's voice.

The woman stands, looking towards the light in the

distance. Turning her head she looks back through the door and sees the last rays of light leaving the valley. In a moment of clarity she feels her heart strengthen. Courage rises within her.

She turns towards the light and walks on. The door closes behind her.

She walks in this abyss for a time, darkness on all sides. Slowly she forgets what she left behind. Her past seems a distant dream, slipping from her grasp. In the empty space that her mind becomes an image appears. It is her, filled with peace and freed from the burdens she carries. There is laughter in her and the slick, clever energy of a natural trickster. She sees further into this vision. It is her when she has found peace. It is her Self. Within it she feels connection, a love for all things. It is a soulful abundance she had forgotten long ago. Her heart yearns to be this person.

The light she had been walking towards, yet that never seemed closer, grows in size. It becomes a blue star in front of her. Its surface is pure fire, roiling and dancing. The vision of her Self is drawn out of her mind's eye and takes shape within the star.

The spirit of her Self that manifests in front of her seems older than her. Wisdom dances behind the spirit's eyes. There is a sly smile on her Self's lips that speaks of playful calculation, of an endless and cosmic irony that only she can see. Within that star, burning bright and with flames dancing on its surface, this image of her Self stands. She emanates a deep, vibrant green set upon a warm darkness. It feels like lush grass growing in fertile soil.

Her past comes rushing back as her mind escapes her. She reflects, in this, her own nature and it calls to her. She sees within herself a great peace, feeling also the burdens that weigh her down in a way she never has before. Growing tired and weary she lifts her weight up. The peace fades. A slight frustration appears beneath her surface, returning from the emptiness her mind became. Looking towards this vision of her Self she finds a point of balance, her center, and is emptied again.

"Why have you come?" The vision asks. The voice is hers, yet beneath it there is a thunder that seems to come from everywhere at once. Her mind whirls. It is as though the voice came also from within her, calling from her center.

The woman takes a moment to compose herself, then speaks: “I seek to know.” Her voice feels distant from her, small in the space of The Temple. She feels that these words are beyond her ability to shape, just as a dream is the dream’s alone to create. It is a spirit coming over her.

“What do you seek to know?” Asks the vision, the smile on her lips broadening. A spark flickers in her eye.

The woman stands for a moment, contemplating this question. She realizes she had never asked it before. ‘What is knowledge?’ She asks herself, ‘why do I seek it?’

“Do you want to know the meaning of life?” speaks the vision, raising her right hand. A seedling appears to the spirit’s right. The seedling grows quickly, maturing into an abundant apple tree. One of the branches stretches itself over to the spirit. An apple grows from it in a moment, hanging in its fullness. The spirit reaches up, plucks the apple from the tree, and tosses it towards the woman.

The woman raises her hands to catch the apple. As soon as she touches it, it turns to smoke. The vision fades.

“Do you want to know how the cosmos works?” The vision raises her left hand. The night sky appears in the darkness to her left. The woman can see celestial bodies orbiting around a star. She sees great beings meditating within them, their image peaceful and filled with meaning. The star explodes, enveloping the solar system in a brilliant light. It is a light unlike any she had ever seen before. She feels the universe break within the vision. The light is drawn back into the heart of the star, taking with it the celestial bodies. For a moment she can see a black hole resting where the star once was. The vision fades.

“Do you want to know who created all things?” The spirit looks up. Above her, from out of no-thing, a mass made of light manifests. Within it the woman sees all things reflected. She sees herself also, within. With a loud crack, echoing in and through all things, the mass of light expands. She sees, in its wave of expansion, that the light weaves with the dark, the two becoming One. As her gaze takes her deeper she sees that vision of her Self smiling from within the Dark-Light. She sees her life, and all life also. She sees the Dark-Light within her. The No-Thing Who is All Things expanding and contracting. She calms herself, watching peacefully.

The vision leaves in a split second. She is back, standing in front of her Self.

"I don't want to know any of these things." She speaks without thinking, without control, urged by a spirit within and beyond her. "They are beautiful and great, yet they do not bring me peace."

The vision of her Self smiles, **"what do you seek to know?"**

"I want to know how to live" She speaks, tears welling in her eyes. "I want to know how to be at peace… I want to be like you."

Love fills the spirit, a glimmer of something greater shining through. **"I am not at peace"** The spirit speaks, yet the voice is no longer her own. It is no-voice and all voices, resonating like thunder in The Temple. **"And so I am."** Her reflection begins to fade. **"It is through this that I have known myself as life."** The voice that is both no voice and all voices resonates through all things. It resounds beyond her and within her, moving through her and with her. The vision of her Self has faded completely. All she sees is the star, speaking Thunder, She sees the spirits of her ancestors dancing in the flames. She sees a great joy within them as they dance around Their fire. **"In all things there is both darkness and light child."** The star becomes Pure Light. Seeing further a Pure Darkness is woven within. **"Should the Light war with the Dark then it is eternal conflict"** She is no longer standing in The Temple. She is standing within her heart. The Dark-Light shines within her, woven into her fabric. **"Truly I am both, as you are"** She stands in her heart, the Dark-Light Star surrounding her and within her, moving through her and with her. Their cold warmth emanates in her memory, always known and reminding her. **"The path is the path, child, and The Way is The Way."**

She wakes at the foot of The Temple. It is morning. The first rays of light awaken the valley. The birds have started singing in the distance. She feels a heartbeat beneath her, reminding her that she is not alone. She remembers her elder and feels the warmth of her elder's touch on her shoulder again, briefly. She lays down for a moment, feeling the world around her. It is peaceful.

She stands, remembering her journey with gratitude and feeling a new sense of rest within her. Before she leaves she walks up to The Temple and touches the door. She feels the Life within it, calling to her with love. She gives thanks, placing her forehead on the door and returning that same love. It is filled with a spirit she thought she had lost, this love she gives. Her heart is both empty and full. She gives thanks once more then speaks a quiet goodbye to The Temple.

As she walks away she looks within and sees that building in her heart, small and unadorned, decorated only with the blooms of old growth. She sees her Self reflected and remembers with love the One who lives within.

Living

"When we measure what we gain by material possession we lose much of what life has to offer."

Creation is more than material. When we measure what we gain by material possession we lose the understanding that experience and energy are also a part of our life. The treasures of 'Heaven' are not material. They are wisdom, peace, Truth, etc… The one who seeks only worldly possessions is possessed by them. All things are borrowed.

"Evil is to live backwards."

To Truly Live, in life's Truth, is also to Know Balance and find peace. To be evil is to choose death. It is to know no Balance and have no peace. Truly to be evil is to live backwards.

"One who cannot be challenged and keep their peace has yet to Know The Way"

Take all things with a grain of salt and a kernel of Truth, seeking first the lesson that takes you towards the fullness of Life.

"To Truly Know is to not know very, very well"

The substantial Truth is incomprehensible. It is for the sake of its very existence that it is beyond knowing. That what we believe is what we know means that all Knowledge is based in the illusion of perception. To empty into fullness then, to become, is to Know. In becoming we become all Knowledge. In becoming we enter the place where all Knowledge exists. It is equanimity, this True Knowledge. It is to not know very well. When one learns to not know they gain the ability to see what is. This sight is True Knowledge. This sight is to not know very, very well. It is that all Knowledge exists in every thing so to Know is to not know, it is to see. It is to become.

Wisdom is the application of Knowledge. To understand the principles of creation is Knowledge, to operate in alignment with them is Wisdom.

It is True Knowledge that expands potential. It is Universal Truth that is the origin of True Knowledge

"Wisdom isn't always wise."

The fullness of wisdom is not rigid, rather it is a fluid acknowledgement of reality. The one who thinks only of their own way of knowing is often blinded to both the misstep that leads to fullness and to the growth of their Way. Wisdom does not say it Knows The Way, rather it asks where The Way leads. In this Wisdom Knows The Way.

"The way forward is not always straight"

At times we must learn to take a way that appears a deviation from our plans to walk the path, as I say, Spirit has given us. The Way that leads to fullness is not always direct, yet it remains that peace is within our reach should we see our Way within us. It is being, and learning to be. It is the True Nature.

You must understand to uplift. To lift a thing up one must stand under it. It cannot be done another way.

Laughter is the best medicine. Humor is sacred. It a face of Creator. As They contemplated Themself They became 'confused' at Their Nature and laughed. Their laughter reconciled Their paradox. What we call 'irony' is also an energetic pattern of creation, reconciling paradoxical relationships. When our brain reconciles a thing we laugh. Creator is always laughing at Themself, then, that They may Know Their folly with joy.

"The integrity of the fool becomes the wisdom of the elder."

The fool who, having taken their missteps, continues their path with True integrity is the one that learns to step into wisdom. This fullness of wisdom is the fool learning to control their folly. Integrity is the fool's best guide. The elder has learned to dance their spirit, and in this it is the fullness of the 'folly' which is Life.

Wisdom does not exist without skill. The one who does not act skillfully has yet to become wise.

Responsibility = the ability to respond.

"The pathway to skill is responsibility"

When a person learns to respond to their environment with ability they are skillful. This skill is also wisdom.

"Abundance knows how to pay its price peacefully"

There is a price given to all things that is its Balance. The one who is innately good hearted also tends to be more inward drawn and doubtful. It is for the same reason that they feel the world around them that this is so. The one who is a speaker tends to easily lead themself into difficult circumstances and does not see the Truth within as easily. There is a price given to all things. Those who know how to pay this price while keeping their peace are the ones whose hearts are abundant. Even in small, momentary actions this reality exists. The one who wants a clean home must learn to pay the price of its keeping. The one who wants to achieve things must learn to pay the price of their achievement. Even the one who must go out in the morning to get coffee because they have none left must learn to do this thing with peace. When we learn to pay our price with peace our heart becomes abundant and abundance becomes a part of us.

"Those who cannot see beyond themself will never find their Self"

Rigid belief in a single way of thought misleads the discerning mind. Who can see beyond the horizon when they have already decided what is beyond it? In Truth it does not matter whether it is one way or another, except that we have found our peace. That peace, which is our place of rest, is also the ability to honor all ways of knowing.

"If what you know does not bring you rest then to shelter in what you know will only ever bring you unrest"

The Wellspring is Eternal, yet to make a trickle a torrent, such is The Way.

"We are not defined by our mistakes but by our will to overcome them"

Forgiveness is a selfish act in a similar way to love being hedonistic. Such is the state of goodness and feeling well that in its purest form it is both selfless and selfish.

"The path to health is a path through sickness."

To create health we must face our sickness. The path leads through overcoming the illness. Such it is that the one who has walked far into the imbalance must walk that same path to return, should they take no detours along The Way.

To be willing to change, to transform, is the gate to finding peace in one's life. Beyond our immediate identity lives a greater Truth. This Truth is our True Nature. When we work towards transformation we move closer to our True Nature innately. The act of transformation is the act of stepping into our Self.

In the game of minds the warrior fights with words.

The warrior is not complete without compassion. The True warrior stands first in their heart and second in the world.

"We must begin at the beginning then take each step one by one, growing as we go."

This may seem a clear and straightforward thought yet so often it is that we veer from it. To understand the importance of this thought is the conception of discipline.

In the darkest depths shine the brightest lights. The weight of our burden is also the strength of our blessing should we rise to meet it.

Everything we are in this moment is a choice we have made at some level of our being. Choice is very Powerful, for Creator chose to create. We may not always perceive the effects of choices we have both made and not made, yet it remains that we are the expression of our choice. This is an empowered Truth. The one who can hone their choice, for this reason, overcomes all obstacles.

"Sometimes I go about in pity for myself and all the while a great wind carries me across the sky"

- Ojibwe saying

To allow ourselves to remain in self-pity is to give away our Power. It is to 'be carried by the wind'.to wherever life takes us. Self-pity is a stone tied around our leg, dragging us into the depths of our despair and drowning us in it.

Even when affected we must be the cause of our salvation.

"The body does not automatically know the spirit."

As one comes into life they forget their Self. The body must be taught of its True Nature in order to remember its Self. We must learn of who we are then teach our body to stand in that True Nature. Our body does not automatically know our spirit, and so we must teach our 'self' to be.

"Self-awareness is a great key to the fullness of life."

"Inward turned sight is the birth of insight"

The one who first turns their gaze inward is the one who remains poised in a good way. This is the one who becomes insightful, for through understanding themself they have come to understand many things beyond them.

To surrender over to Spirit is not a giving of one's life, it is a giving of one's death. This is the purest of self-sacrifice. To surrender to Spirit is a giving over to Purpose that one may Live without death controlling them.

We are on the journey of a thousand lifetimes. What, then, is Purpose?

Every person is given a fire to tend. This fire is the fire of our ancestors. It is the fire of our spirit and soul. It is the fire of our Purpose. To keep our fire is to fan our divine spark and shine our Light along The Way. To keep our Fire is to hold our Lantern high.

Every great work is accomplished with small steps, direct actions, and a strong foundation.

"It is when we stop giving thanks for what we have that we truly lose everything."

There is an energetic quality to gratitude that manifests abundance. The one who remembers their blessings turns their sight to good things and sets the energy of creation to bless them. In the cosmic horizon it is that one who in the darkest of nights remembers the dawn brings it closer.

Life is a learning opportunity.

There is a natural resistance to new ways of living that we must learn to acknowledge and overcome. This 'resistance' is a form of memory that is meant to help create structure in our unconscious. It is a product of our unconscious structuring how we relate to the world around us. It is an aspect of conditioning that lets us find rest in our Way. To overcome this 'body memory' is fluid pathway when we are walking in our True Nature, yet it remains a presence that can feel 'heavy'. It is wise to acknowledge this presence as we seek a better life, that we may understand what we are facing. The will to overcome is also the will to be.

To Live is to rise above our fear and come to know our life beyond it. True courage overcomes its 'self'.

It is about who we are more than what we are. We are human, not what-man

"When you give no space to make a choice you give no space to not choose it"

At an unconscious level when a person gives no space for a choice to be made they limit the fullness of their heart's expression. It is a different feeling to make the choice not to when we understand that the choice is ours to make. To make the choice not to do a thing is a healing work in which we realize the value of our life beyond the choice we have to make. The one who does not give room to a choice is denying a substantial reality. It is that the choice exists. When the heart is given no room to understand the choice it has to make it cannot understand its True choice. The True Nature is free, and loves Balance and freedom. The True Nature does not destroy its Self, for it understands the value of Life. When you give no room for a choice to be made you leave no room to not choose it.

"Eventually we all must grieve the life we thought we wanted in favor of our Purpose."

We all dream as youth. Our dreams are what bring us passion and define us. Eventually we all must grieve these dreams so that we may learn to meet life with peace. It is not that we lose these dreams that we grieve them. It is that we learn to acknowledge the fullness of Life with peace through grieving them. Even those who succeed in achieving their dreams must grieve them to find their rest. The one who doesn't grieve the life they thought they wanted will find themself always searching. What they seek exists within them. It is for the reason that Life is not our own dream, but the dream of All. The one who doesn't grieve the life they thought they wanted, even in success, may find their fullness beyond them still. It is that we step into the fullness of our dream that we grieve the life we thought we wanted. Our Purpose is a calling from Life. Until we can step into that calling and into Life we will struggle to find a place of rest.

"The one that forsakes the journey forsakes the goal"

The Golden Rules

These four golden rules can help to orient a person on good living.

"Do Unto All Else as You Would Have Done Unto Yourself, and Unto Yourself Do The Same"

To do to others as one would have done to themself is a powerful way of maintaining healthy living. This golden rule, however, extends to all our relations. We must do to all else as we would have done to ourself. In this we may perceive a deeper and more profound Truth. It is that one is not another. The tree is not the human, yet the tree's Life is valuable. In this, then, we must be present in a way that understands how we would want to be treated if we were in another person's place. A person would not gain by treating a tree as though it was a human. A person would gain by understanding how to respect the trees in their place in creation. A person would not gain by treating someone who is sick as though they are healthy. A person with a broken leg should likely not be expected to walk. To do to 'all else' as we would have done to ourself, then, is also to understand how we would want to be treated if we were in the others place. As we look into the Natural world this understanding helps us uphold our place within our environment. As we look into our community this understanding helps us uphold that good respect that brings Life into the world.

This golden rule continues to say 'and unto yourself do the same'. Our ability to respect others is a reflection of our ability to respect ourself. The one who does not respect themself will struggle to respect others in a way that is full. Within their unconscious they would not feel well, and so they would struggle to uphold that good respect. A person, then, must do unto themself as they would have done unto themself. This part of the golden rule, even, extends into how we would want to treat ourself in the immediate state of our existence. A person with a broken leg should not disrespect themself because they cannot walk. When we do not treat ourself with respect we lose our ability to uphold our place in creation. Our ability to show respect is a reflection of the respect we show ourself.

"Persist in the Work of Learning To Act with Responsibility"

Responsibility is the ability to respond. To learn to be responsible, through good response, is to learn how to live a full life. To persist, always, towards learning to be responsible is to poise oneself on good living. Life is more complex than always having good response. A person, however, who persists in the work of learning to respond well will remain poised in good living. In this responsibility we may perceive a deeper reality. The one who does not walk their healing journey in response to carrying suffering has not worked with their burdens and suffering responsibly. The one who does not seek their Way has not acted responsibly in relation to their Self. The one who does not remember why to respect has not acted responsibly in learning the value of Life. To persist in the work of learning to act responsibly, then, is also a thing of awareness. To persist in learning responsibility, even if one has learned good responsibility, keeps one poised in a place of fullness.

"Do Your Best To Live in a Full Way"

To live fully is a place of rest. To do one's best is to live fully. To do one's best to live, then, is a restful place, or at least leading to a restful place. To do one's best to live fully is to seek the place of rest. To do our best is not only about succeeding in an endeavor. It is about living in the way that fulfills the spirit within us.

"Turn Towards What Brings You Peace"

We are created to find peace in the fullness of our life. We are created to find peace when we are healthy, full, and doing what we are here to do. The True Nature within us is given a Purpose. It is when we have followed our Purpose, while also maintaining our fullness, that we find our peace. Where we have found our peace is also where we uphold the fullness of the life that is around us. It is a self-reflection, a spiral pattern, that occurs. We must turn towards our peace, then, to be able to uphold our place in creation. The one who has searched for their peace is also the one who can keep peace with the world. Where for one this peace is one thing, for another it will be another thing.

The Three Essential Logics

There are three essential logics in all people. These three essential logics express from origin and become fundamental variables in the way of operation of all people. These are: The Primal Logic, The Divine Logic, and The Self's Logic. All people have within them these three forms of logic.

The Primal Logic

The primal logic is an innate part of our unconscious reasoning that seeks to motivate us through what pleases us. The primal logic motivates through what pleases, however is capable of not seeing far enough to understand what Truly does. It is peace that pleases this logic the most. It is the logic within us that says 'eat when you are hungry' and 'drink when you are thirsty'. When we are unwell and do not understand the value of what we are doing this logic says: 'consume until it breaks you' and 'do not fulfill your needs'.

Awareness

When a person does not understand what Truly pleases them, such as eating healthy or being consistently physically active, the primal logic can seek its own destruction. It is not Truly seeking destruction, this logic, rather it is seeking life in ignorance of what it means to live. When a person is not aware enough to understand the True effect of an action the primal logic can become an urge of self-destruction. It is not the True Nature of the primal logic to destroy itself, rather it is an expression of illness within a person.

Suffering

The primal logic often becomes destructive when a person carries suffering. In order to ease the suffering of a person their primal logic will seek transient pleasure. In this way the primal logic may seek its own destruction. Our primal logic drives us to ease our dis-ease, however its True Nature is Life.

The Divine Logic

The divine logic seeks to uphold the Spirit, however often forgets its own needs. This logic sees far, and often forgets what is directly in front of it. This logic is one that fulfills us. It is within the divine logic that one seeks to give and is fulfilled in giving.

Giving

Within the divine logic a person may give until they do not have enough to fulfill their needs. A person may feel strongly that they must, even up to the point where they give away what brings them peace. Our own peace is also the peace of the world.

Dogma

The divine logic is capable of becoming dogmatic in relation to its ideas of what is right. A person who has focused strongly on the divine logic may develop rigidity in their ideas that, to them, matter more than the fullness of life. When this occurs a person becomes capable of evil.

The Self's Logic

The Self's logic is the logic of our innate individuality. Within our unconscious we are always reasoning in relation to the nature of our Self. We all look into the world and, within our unconscious, measure what we see against the nature of our Self

To find the fullness of the Spirit we must work with all three essential logics. The one who gives heedlessly empties their spirit of its needs; the one who consumes heedlessly fills their spirit with poison; the one who does not uphold their Self becomes lost. The one who contemplates within themself the fullness of their life, knowing they are both the sacred primal and the sacred divine, finds the Balance of the True Nature. It is this Balance that knows peace, regardless of ideology. It is the Balance between the primal instinct and the divine nature that brings 'Heaven' to Earth. It is Unity, being the coming together of all things.

"Gazing too long into the sun will blind a person as surely as standing too long in the darkness."

"The Dark holds all the things that the Light can't bear."

Within the 'fundamental Dark' is kept the suffering and burdens that we have yet to work with. Our primal logic is an expression of the essential 'Darkness' of our being. Our suffering becomes the 'evil' that is often perceived as the nature of the primal logic. Our suffering is kept with our primal logic. Our primal logic then expresses in relation to our suffering. It is not the nature of the primal to be evil, for our instincts are human. It is the nature of the primal to live, yet we may forget how to. Within our primal Dark our suffering is kept. This becomes the evil that is often associated with the nature of the primal logic.

The Nature of Suffering

Much like the body bleeds, the spirit suffers. When we are wounded our spirit, our energetic expression, releases suffering. The nature of suffering is energetic poison expressing from wounds kept within our unconscious. Suffering, in this way, is the loss of life. We are not designed to suffer, rather suffering is energetic sickness.

"Suffering is energetic poison"

When we are wounded our spirit releases an energetic poison we call suffering. The energetic poison fills our unconscious and affects us. In this way our wounds affect us.

"Suffering is spiritual sickness"

When the energetic poison of suffering is able to integrate into the unconscious a person becomes sick spiritually. The energetic nature of a person integrates processes and patterns that reinforce the pain they have experienced. A person, then, has processes within their unconscious that consistently reinforce their suffering. This is the loss of the True Nature.

"A person with much suffering has room for little else"

One cannot be blamed for bleeding when they are cut. One cannot be blamed for being affected when they are abused. The spirit and the heart may also bleed, and these wounds are easier to become infected than the body's.

The Expressions of Suffering

Suffering will always seek a way to express. Suffering causes the unconscious to compensate in destructive ways. The unconscious, having come to carry suffering, seeks to sustain the suffering in various ways. These various ways that the unconscious compensators for the presence of suffering are The Expressions of Suffering.

Common Expressions of Suffering include: *Division, Control, Absence, Abuse, Malaise Disempowerment, Attachment,* and *Addiction.*

Division

A person with suffering will seek a focal point in the world to focus their pain on. They will divide, and this becomes hate. It is rarely about what a person hates so much as that they have a thing to ease their heart of its dis-ease. This is why it is often said: 'people will always find something to hate'. It is an expression of suffering that we divide.

Control

Control is power-centric. It is the need to have power over or control of your surroundings. When a person expresses suffering in this way, to lose that control can provoke fear. Through control a person eases the sense that they are not well. They can feel 'in control' instead of powerless.

Absence

Absence is the will to leave the world behind. A person with suffering may feel the need to leave the world. To leave the world eases them. The one who is absent has had their spirit leave this world. Their suffering has driven them away from life.

Abuse

A person with suffering may abuse another to feed from their life-force. Their spirit takes from the life-force of another in order to satisfy its dis-ease. The one who abuses another is ill. Suffering will often seek to put another down to ease the emotional pain. It is to fill the space of the emptiness at the expense of others

.

Malaise

A person with suffering may lose all will to do anything. Their unconscious may compensate for the presence of suffering by losing the will to act and live.

Disempowerment

A person with suffering may express that suffering as disempowerment. Their unconscious may process the suffering as reasons to not feel well about itself. He suffering processes within them, making disempowerment seem justified.

Attachment

A person with suffering may seek people, activities, or objects in their surrounding to attach to. A person who has attached in a way that eases their suffering would feel that to lose that thing would be like dieing. The one who eases their suffering with attachment has attached the meaning of their life to the object of their attention

Addiction

The use of external forces to sustain energetically is addiction. Suffering will often seek a form of consumption to ease its emotional pain. The heart will then continuously be driven to consume so it does not need to feel unwell. A person with addiction has found a way to sustain himself energetically through means external to them.

We all express suffering in our own way. Where one person may be more drawn to absence and addiction, another may be more drawn to control and abuse. The way we express suffering is our own. When we understand how we express our suffering it helps us understand the reasoning behind our behavior. In this way we gain a greater ability to overcome suffering. When we carry the spiritual sickness of suffering it will seek to express. To understand our expressions of suffering is to gain Power over it.

The Expressions of Suffering are not the only ways suffering may express. When we carry suffering our unconscious seeks to ease its burden through destructive means. The Expressions of Suffering are common ways that suffering may express, however they are not the only.

Compensation

When we offer no room for suffering to express and do not walk our healing journey our unconscious may compensate for the suffering we have within us. Our unconscious may make us sick as a way to express the energy we are holding. A person, for instance, may get a stomach ache or a headache when they stop expressing suffering, and if they do not walk their healing journey. This is a natural action of the unconscious. Our unconscious must express our suffering or release it. This action of the unconscious is capable of making a person physically sick.

"We are not our suffering"

Our True Nature, our foremost and fullest expression in this life, is not our suffering. Suffering steals away our True Nature. We are not our suffering. Within the cosmic equations that are the binding constructs of creation we are not our suffering. Suffering steals away our True Nature, our Oneness, and makes us forget. We are the wind and water, the fire and earth. Our True Nature is free of suffering. It is only that we have lost that seed of Truth that we do not know it.

Seeds of Imbalance

When we take in destructive beliefs we plant seeds of imbalance. A seed of imbalance creates processes within our unconscious that create suffering within us. When we are seeking to release our suffering we must be conscious of what beliefs exist within our unconscious mind. If we do not tend to the seeds we plant we will not reap an abundant harvest.

A seed of imbalance is a destructive belief. Our thoughts form in relation to our beliefs. When we believe in destructive ways we will have destructive thoughts. When we believe in our own defeat we will always be defeated. This is a way that suffering is created. It is within our Power to change these destructive processes within us. The True Nature does not believe in its own defeat, nor does it believe in its destruction.

Three examples of seeds of imbalance are: *Abuse, Torment,* and *Possession/Domination*

Abuse

Abuse, as a seed of imbalance, is the product of an unconscious death wish. It is the choice of imbalance. This choice is made, for the most part, at an unconscious level. This choice expresses into our unconscious, becoming suffering and affecting our way of operation. The choice of imbalance expresses into ways of behaving that create imbalance. The creation of imbalance becomes abuse, both personal and communal. A person who has an unconscious death wish has within their unconscious the seed of imbalance called abuse. The seed of imbalance that is abuse is always born of suffering, and will always keep suffering with a person. We must believe in the value of life beyond suffering in order to overcome this seed.

Torment

When we cannot see ourself well we torment ourself. We become tormented for our inability to perceive ourself well. A person who believes they are unworthy is tormented within themself. They become the vision of themself that is tormented. They take in unconscious processes that create destructive thoughts. The internal torment becomes suffering. The one who is tormented becomes one who brings imbalance into the world. A person who seeks to overcome torment must learn to honor their Truth and step into their Self. Unconditional love, that does not justify the loss of the True Nature, is a great key for overcoming this seed of imbalance.

Possession/Domination

Possession and domination are power-centric. As a person has lost their Personal Power they gain this seed of imbalance. This seed expresses in two ways. The first expression of this seed is victimhood. A person enters into victimhood and becomes possessed by their surroundings. The second expression is domination. A person, in the loss of their Power, becomes obsessed with having control over. They become one who needs that control, yet it is because they have lost their Power. When we have lost our Personal Power we gain within us this seed of imbalance. This seed then expresses within our unconscious reasoning, creating destructive thought patterns.

To free ourself from suffering we must work to change the unconscious processes that keep us sick. The one who has planted the seed of abuse must learn to choose life. The one who has planted the seed of torment must learn to see themself well and with unconditional love. The one who has planted a seed of possession/domination must reclaim their Personal Power. We must tend to the seeds we plant, for our unconscious is a garden.

It is wise to gather healing tools that we know help us release our suffering. To find actions that work well to release our suffering is a powerful way to maintain the fullness of our life. A person may go to therapy or speak to a trusted friend. A person may find time in nature or physical activity healing. A person may find journaling or meditation very healing. To have healing tools we know work well for us creates a great difference in quality of life. To have a few healing tools that we know we can turn to is an important part of maintaining a full life.

"Suffering is the destroyer of worlds"

The Power of Suffering

Suffering carries three powers within it. These powers are: *Forgetting, Blindness,* and *Evil*

Forgetting:

Suffering causes a person to forget. It is a natural survival mechanism that a person forgets when they come to carry suffering. They forget to survive. As a person becomes wounded they may forget what fullness looks like so they are not reminded of their loss. In this way they become able to survive.

Blindness:

When a person forgets there is a blindness that occurs within them. It is this blindness that allows them to express their suffering in destructive ways. They forget and go blind. They do not see what they are doing. If they saw what they were doing they could no longer forget. If they no longer forgot they would be urged into their healing journey. They would see, even, that which is within them if they were not blind to it. Suffering causes blindness. T is this blindness that allows the expression of suffering.

Evil:

Suffering is the origin of evil. As a person comes to carry great suffering it alters them. They forget and go blind. As they become very forgetful they become very blind. Their soul leaves them and the space becomes filled with the potential for evil. Suffering is the origin of evil.

"The justification of suffering is universal"

When we justify suffering we blind our Sacred Heart. We blind our innermost Truth within that justification. When we justify, even, the suffering of those seemingly opposed to us we become blind to Truth. Suffering is universal. The justification of suffering is also universal. It becomes our own suffering, for we are all One.

"Suffering is the True death"

Suffering is the death of the soul. It is the loss of Life. A person may die in this world and live in the next. A person may be dead in this life, and in all worlds that come. It is suffering that is this True death.

"One should not fear death, rather they should fear choosing death"

There is nothing better to hate than hate itself. If one must hate a thing, for suffering will always find its way, then hate the ways of suffering, of evil, that the spirit within may remain poised in Truth.

"The one who seeks peace will find abundance, for within the heart of the peaceful exists the seed of True wealth."

Relaxation is a powerful tool when working to release suffering. When we learn to maintain our relationship with relaxation we push against suffering and the integrated stress that holds suffering in place. When we push to create a good relationship with relaxation we also create the opportunity for healing. The wounds that hold our suffering, and stress, in place begin to release their attachment to suffering. A good way to learn to maintain our relationship with relaxation is by consistently using relaxation techniques. A good and simple relaxation technique is to go to where we keep our stress in our body and consciously help the muscles release the tension.

"Peace is a choice"

To turn towards peace is a choice we must make as individuals. It is a powerful choice within us when it is made Truly. A person who chooses peace Truly chooses the Truth of life. They walk a path towards the fullness of their life. We must turn towards what brings us peace, and this is also a healing journey.

"Peace breeds peace"

"Peace is the most pleasing of states if one knows how to find it"

Peace is found in alignment with Natural Law. A person who is aligned with Natural Law lives in the fullness of their life. It is our True Nature, our Self. It is a state of integrative health. Peace occurs when the soul has found rest within us. This state of being is individual and universal. It is the fullness of our own in alignment with the energetic principles of creation. Truly, by Natural Law, the fullness of our own could not occur except within this alignment. In this, peace is bound by the principles of Oneness, for all things return to Oneness in their most essential nature. A person, then, who does not uphold equality will sacrifice their potential for peace so that they may be divided. A person who does not respect the principles of Oneness could neither achieve peace, nor could they achieve the fullness of their own. There is a great difference in quality of life between the one who upholds the universal and the one who does not. A person who reaches that state of peace would naturally become one who upholds the principles of Oneness, even if they did not intend to. Peace is the most pleasing of states. It occurs when our soul has found rest within us. This state of being is individual and universal. It is our own in alignment with the Natural Laws of creation.

The Medicine Wheel

Body, Mind, Spirit, and Emotions are an indigenous teaching offered to me through Annishinaabe and Sami teachings.

There are four main parts of the human being. The four main parts of our being are: Body, Mind, Spirit, and Emotion. They are expressions of the four primordial elements; fire, earth, air, and water. Within the elementary particle these Powers are: first power, mass, interconnection/potential, and waveform. Through understanding these aspects of our being we may learn to align with the substantial energetic nature of creation and gain clarity regarding how to live a full life.

Body is the Sacred Vessel; Earth; Mass; Solid

Our body is a biological 'robot' that our spirit and soul inhabit. It is the sacred vessel that allows us to exist within the material world. A healthy body upholds its needs, respects its place in the world, and learns to keep Balance. A healthy body comes to know its spirit. To work with the body is to cultivate our Earth.

In order to uphold our body we must:

Be Conscious of Consumption
Maintain Physical Capacity
Respect Environment

Mind is the Sacred Vehicle; Air; Interconnection/Potential; Gas

Our mind is the sacred vehicle of our consciousness. It is the vehicle of the soul and spirit. A healthy mind structures our existence, channeling our wind into creation. An unhealthy mind is untethered, carried by its winds and without substance. To work with the mind is to create structure for our Wind.

In order to uphold our mind we must:

Tend our Inner-Garden, our Unconscious
Build Mental Structure in Relation to The World
Develop Ability

Spirit is the Sacred Expression; Fire; Life-Force; Sublimation

The spirit is the energetic expression of our individuality that exists within us. Our spirit is what drives us to exist as individuals. A healthy spirit has found its True Nature and knows its Way well. It keeps its Fire, tending its divine spark and feeding its flames. An unhealthy spirit is confused. It has not found its Self and so finds nothing everywhere. To work with the spirit is to tend and feed our Fire.

In order to uphold our spirit we must:

Create Routine and Structure that Upholds our Self
Tend your Fire
Let Go of Attachments and Suffering

Emotion is the Sacred Relationship; Water; Waveform; Liquid

Emotion is the soul's relationship with the world. Our emotions are the energetic response of our soul occurring within our unconscious. Emotional health is a fluid upholding of the purpose of emotions. When our emotions are healthy they become a fluid relationship with the world around us. Emotion is the savor of life. To work with emotion is to tend our Water and become ceaseless in our Way.

In order to uphold our emotions we must:

Learn to Observe our Emotions
Be Consistent in Relation to Emotions
Honor the Nature and Purpose of Emotions

These four aspects are represented in the Medicine Wheel of Indigenous traditions. It is that, though they share one circle, they are also each their own circle. There is a spirit within the body that is the body's. It is the energy body. There is a mind within emotion that is the emotion's. It is the emotional logic. There is a mind within the body that is the body's. It is the subconscious. Each circle overlaps within us. This is our immediate being.

Two Monks and a River

It was a day where clouds were almost all one could see of the sky and quiet seemed the thought of Mother Earth. There was a river that ran between a Christian and a Buddhist monastery. It came from the mountains and passed all the way to the ocean. The current ran slow on this day, as though calmed by the earth's Silence.

One monk from both monasteries had a thought to walk to the river as they were in their morning practices. Both had spent many years in their search for their respective forms of enlightenment. The first, a Christian, had prayed holes into the knees of his gown, calling for The Father to be revealed to him. The other, a Buddhist monk, had meditated countless hours seeking Nirvana. They both arrived at the river around the same time and sat at the river's bank. The sound of the water and the soft whisper of the wind passing through the trees soothed their souls. A sacred Silence overtook them.

It wasn't long after the Silence came that the clouds parted in the sky. A ray of light shone through. Both were in awe. Within the parting they both saw a sacred image. The Christian monk saw the image of a throne upon which sat a great and powerful man. The Buddhist monk saw the image of a Buddha smiling down upon them.

"Why have you come here? It is peace you seek" spoke the vision. They both heard it as a whisper on the wind, echoing in their minds. There was a slight hint of glee and trickery in the voice.

The image disappeared and the clouds closed. Both monks sat for a moment, astounded.

The Christian monk began to pray, praising God and His divine mercy. The Buddhist monk began meditating, contemplating what they had just experienced. After some time they both stood and walked along the bank. They walked along opposite sides of the river, continuing their prayers and contemplation. Soon, and with a glancing look they passed each other, both acknowledging the other for a brief moment.

The Buddhist monk came to believe that the words were meant to remind them of their connection with all things. They understood that compassion and connection were intertwined. They decided to seek a better understanding of their connection with the world around them.

The Christian monk began searching within for why they went to the river that day, seeking prayer to guide them. They thought only of the beauty of nature and how it had always called to them. Their heart called that nature was also a face of God. They felt within that calling what they searched for in their prayers. It was in their connection to nature. They decided they were meant to develop a stronger connection with nature in order to fulfill the will of God.

In the Heavens God sat next to Buddha laughing to Themself.

Both monks returned to their monasteries. The Christian monk determined to connect with nature; The Buddhist determined to understand connection itself.

Over the years both came to their respective forms of enlightenment and both became One with their Truth.

The Christian monk found that nature sparked a passion in their heart. That passion brought them closer to God than their prayers ever did. They came to understand their time in nature as prayer. They found that God was just as much in the plants, animals, and stones as in the church. They began walking holes in their shoes, finding that they could hear the voice of God carried on the wind. In them blossomed a deep love for creation. In that love they found what they had always searched for. It brought them peace. That day by the river began a journey to a deep and unconditional love for All within themself. It was a love they had only glimpsed before that day at the river.

Looking back years later the Christian monk remembers that voice echoing in their mind. They feel the voice laughing warmly, with love beneath the words. They remember also, clear as the day before, the monk on the other side of the river, walking in the opposite direction.

The Buddhist monk turned their mind towards their conne-

-ction with creation. They meditated on how they connect to the world around them and found a sense of absence within themself. As they continued their meditations they found a feeling of longing and resentment for those who don't seem to care. Eventually the monk came to a heart of peace within themself. In their meditations they came to understand why they were not connecting with true compassion. Over time the light in their heart filled the space of their longing and resentment. They came to understand it was also their origin, this place called peace. They understood that everything in creation has Buddha-Nature in this way. A passion grew in their heart and they began to understand Nirvana in a deeper, more personal, way. Over time the monk became a teacher and found great comfort in watching their students learn.

Looking back years later the Buddhist monk remembers the day at the river and the voice carried on the wind. In their memory the voice is laughing with a deep love beneath the words. They also remember, clear as the day before, the monk on the other side of the river, walking in the opposite direction.

The Garden

Our world is a garden
Within, every belief is a seed
Expanding upon what we plant
Until bearing fruit of like kind,
We may cultivate the fruits of peace and abundance
Should we keep our Garden well

Our Truth is a garden well kept
We are keepers of the world as keepers of our self
So too are we kept, in this place
Walking The Garden in life
It is The Garden of Heaven in All, in I

That my garden may cultivate me
As I have cultivated it
This is Balance
The spiral reflecting in generation for generations
So I keep my garden, The Garden of All
I learn its ways, The Way itself
The study of Nature and Natural Law
The study of Self, the cosmos

I have seen
That even where All returns to One we must learn to keep our garden well
This is the True Nature of Self
We are One made flesh
At the End, where the Beginning begins
It is from our garden we keep our life
And from our life we keep all life
And from all life we keep ourselves
So I keep my garden and my garden keeps me
I keep my life and my life keeps me
I keep all life and all life keeps me
I keep my garden and all life keeps me

This is Heaven's Garden
This is the state of The Shining Ones
Existing in all things to be
The stance of the spiritual warrior
It begins as the gardener
Whose inner-world is a soil, nurturing Truth
Whose thoughts are seeds, contemplating Truth
Whose patterns are cultivated, honoring Truth
Whose ways are measured, aligned with Truth
And bearing fruit in life, that we may live in Truth
The state of Heaven, of Unity, is to cultivate our garden
It is The Garden itself, this cultivation
And creation is the garden of Creator, cultivating Themself
All is One

Nature and Mother Earth

All of life is sacred.

We are the spirit and the animal. The animal of Spirit; the spirit animal.

Humanity is the youngest species on Mother Earth. The plants, animals, and elements are our Grandfathers and Grandmothers

Every tree is a Buddha, every blade of grass enlightened

The spirit of Earth is a stand for Balance. This stand is about one's own integrity as much as it is about honoring and respecting all our relations. It is a stand that is to become the spirit of Balance that lives within.

"The pursuit of Balance is the origin of wisdom"

There is a spirit within us all that is the spiritual warrior. It is 'the one who stands'. The spiritual warrior stands as the oak in the storm. They may bend in the wind, yet they do not break. The will of the spiritual warrior exists within all people. The oak endures just as the spiritual warrior endures.

There is an inherent responsibility that humans carry in their relationship with Mother Earth. This relationship includes our community. We are responsible for our place in this world for the same reason that we are co-creators. We have a relationship with Mother Earth, with the land and all our relations, that we must acknowledge and honor. When we forget this innate responsibility we lose our capacity for peace. To Know this responsibility is also to Know how to keep our place in this world.

Personal Power is the natural state. It is that the disempowered have lost their Natural spirit that they remain in disempowerment.

We are all children of Mother Earth. We are all children of Creator

We are all indigenous to somewhere. Our connection to Mother Earth is within us. Within this connection lives, also, our interconnection with all things. Within this connection lives the Balance of all creation.

All natural forces have a spirit. Their energetic manifestation is their spirit. Humans, similarly, have a spirit, an energetic manifestation. It is an expression of an essential energetic reality of creation. It is energetic manifestation within Universal Consciousness of Creator. The celestial bodies have 'personalities' that reflect their energetic nature. It is their spirit. Mother Earth is also alive in this way. The elements, plants, and animals have spirits. Their nature forms a 'personality' that reflects their place in creation. It is an expression of Spirit. The spirit of Water is a sacred elemental whose consciousness exists in a Timeless Place. The spirit of Cedar is sacred, standing in the prayer that is their life. The spirit of Crow is sacred, moving in alignment with the nature of their spirit. All things in nature have a spirit, an energetic manifestation, that is also their personality. This is a sacred reality and an aspect of their life, just as our spirit is an aspect of our own.

All plants, animals, and elements have a spirit and an energetic medicine. Their medicine is the qualities of their spirit expressing as an energetic resonance. When we hold a crystal we connect to the energetic resonance of its spirit. When we burn a plant we release its medicine into the air. When we place a plant we bring its resonance into the place we put it in. There is a spiritual, energetic, resonance in all things. The medicine of plants, animals, and elements is their spiritual resonance.

All energies resonate in a similar way to harmonics. A person who carries anger will resonate the energy of anger. A person nearby may experience the state of the other's anger, even without conscious awareness. All things exist within an energetic equilibrium, constantly harmonizing to their surroundings. The medicine of the plants, animals, and elements resonates harmonically within the energetic equilibrium of creation.

A person who is attuned to spiritual reality, Spirit, is more likely to experience spiritual, energetic, realities. The part of their brain that is able to experience these realities is developed to a greater degree than the one who is not attuned to the unseen. A person who is not attuned to Spirit is unlikely to experience spiritual realities. The part of their brain that is able to tune into the energetic realities of creation is not developed, and so they will not be able to experience Spirit when the movement is not very powerful. The one who is not attuned to spiritual, energetic, realities will likely gain little from holding a crystal in their hand while the one who is attuned may gain much.

Nature has a voice, as do all her children. It is soul speech. The plants, animals, and elements understand our hearts.

There was a park that I would often walk through near my home. Every day I would enter the park I would pray and give Tobacco to a Grandfather Tree near the park's entrance. One day, as I prayed and gave my Tobacco, the Grandfather Tree spoke. Taken deeper into my Silence my inner-eye saw an orb of light surrounding the silhouette of a person. The Grandfather, filled with love and light, spoke: "I will see you in the Ocean of Spirit". The silhouette of the man dissolved into the light. It was with much love that this Grandfather spoke. One day, when I pass from this world, I will dissolve into the Light and greet that Grandfather's spirit with much love. All is One.

Unconditional Love is the language of Mother Earth. Soul speech is carried upon the vibration of unconditional love.

Elements, plants, and animals speak. They speak in senses and images. When one can listen well these senses become words. Many spirits and greater beings also speak in this way.

The trees have spirits that are their own. They are the standing people. Their life is a song of praise to creation and to Creator. Their life is a light-filled dream.

Our ancestors walk with us. We are their living embodiment.

The blessings and burdens of our ancestors are carried in their spirit, passing on through the generations. This expresses in our blood memory. To do our own healing work is also to help the spirits of our ancestors heal and find peace.

The fullness of our own Light shines in the spirit of our ancestry.

All peoples are given a fire to tend. That fire is Their/their Light. Within every lineage there is the spark of a great fire. We are all lenses through which the Light may shine. All is One.

As I prayed, journeying in the Spirit, a vision appeared. My great great grandfather and great great grandmother stood together, looking towards me. The ocean was behind them and the land around them was that which we now call Nova Scotia. There was love in them as they saw me. It was a rest that, in the Sacred Silence, spoke of a peace that they had not known before my healing work. I gave thanks, then, for this healing work I do. I gave thanks for their rest and the vision of their love. I held love for my ancestors reminding them that I remember them.

"All things are borrowed."

Nothing is owned. One day our body will return to Mother Earth to nourish Her. One day our soul will return to Source and we will be as One with the Ocean. It is folly to think that land is ours. Mother Earth will outlast us all. It is folly to think, even, that we are our own, for we have borrowed our Life from Them-Who-Created-All. Not one can own the air, neither can they put a flag on Truth.

The spirit, the energetic expression, of a person may journey naturally. It is a natural occurrence that is, in the modern world, often associated with madness and illness. We are spirits who walk in matter. To walk with Spirit is our natural state. When a person journeys their spirit travels. It feels like entering a dream or experiencing moments of clarity. To journey is a natural occurrence that was understood as common and sacred in indigenous traditions. It is not madness and it is not illness. When we perceive it as illness it often becomes illness. In indigenous ways of knowing, journeying was expected to occur with all people.

It is natural to experience journeys when we pray. It is the Spirit of Creation reaching for us to help us know our Way.

Those who naturally journey will likely need to learn to keep a stronger foundation than others who are not called to journey. The one who naturally journeys may need to integrate traditional wisdom teachings and fundamental practices in order to sustain a full life. The gift of being called to journeying can become difficult when not kept in balance. Illness occurs when we do not learn to maintain balance in our life. When a person who is called to journey does not have wisdom teachings and fundamental spiritual practices their gift may become much more difficult to bear.

Cleansing prayers and rituals are powerful tools for remaining in a healthy way.

Traditional wisdom teachings are also fundamental internal processes that help us remain stable in our life.

One must always return from a journey, re-entering the body and immediate life. This completes the circle of a journey. It is wise to re-enter through the top of one's head.

General Health (Mental, Physical, Spiritual, Emotional) is key to learning to journey as a practice.

In indigenous traditions it is often that the children would be taught fundamental tools as they grew into adulthood. These tools often included wisdom teachings, fundamental practices, ways of understanding their Self, and ways of understanding their relationship with the world. This teaching work is a way that the stories, traditions, and medicine of the community would be shared with their children. The wisdom of the community would be offered to the child from an early age to help them grow and live a good life. Many of the teaching tools, such as the Medicine Wheel, are very sacred and hold great spiritual value.

We are spirits that walk in matter. It is natural that our inner-eye should see beyond the veil when we have not closed ourselves off. Those who journey are connecting, through their spirit, to worlds beyond our own. It is a sacred and Powerful thing. Those who journey are experiencing the unconscious of creation through their energetic interconnection.

'Psychoactive' medicines often cause the spirit to journey. Without wisdom it is easy to become lost in No Man's Land, the space between life and death.

What we call spiritual realities were once a common and well understood aspect of life. It was not 'supernatural' to experience spiritual realities. It was natural.

In old ways the healers and medicine people would journey to learn to work with Spirit, and the spirits, that they may aid their community. There were often works that a member of the community could take part in if they chose. These works were highly regarded and known to be very difficult works. As they learned the medicine ways the medicine person would also learn to be keepers of the wisdom and stories of their nation.

Spirit is in all things. Spirit is the energetic expression of creation. Spirit is the Spirit of Creation. One cannot separate from this Truth. We are spirits who walk in matter. A person who does not know their spirit has lost their humanity. Spirit is not a doctrine. Spirit is a part of all life.

In many indigenous traditions there were considered to be those who were gifted to walk the paths of Spirit. When a person who was considered to be born for the medicine work would appear in community they would be given to a medicine person or elder to train. These 'gifted ones' often hear and see naturally. Their gift, however, is also considered a weight that they must bear. It is that they struggle to live as others do for the sake of their spiritual gifts. In the modern world those who would have been considered gifted for the medicine work are often considered ill. They are often treated as being ill and so become ill. In the old ways they would have been considered sacred and taught to keep their gift.

When I was 12 I received my first vision and began hearing. It came to me as I went into the shower, turned off the lights, and lay down to listen to the running water. I became a Crow, flying through the air. I experienced flight then, and it was beautiful. Having flown for a time I dived into the ground and came to in a vast emptiness as my child self. I saw, then, Crow rise above two sets of totems with wings spread. It was hawk and bear. It was rhino and lion. Crow looked down towards me, as I stood in my child self, and said: 'you are not ready'. Crow has been my Grandfather and guide ever since.

I am taught that in a traditional indigenous community I would have been given to train in the medicine ways. Having received my first vision at the age of 12 would have meant that I am gifted for the works of Spirit. I would have apprenticed under a medicine person or elder to learn how to keep balance in relation to my gift.

Medicine is the inherent Power existing in all things. Medicine work is the spiritual discipline of learning to work with the inherent Power of creation.

Sitting in conversation with a friend the Spirit took me. I drifted through a blinding light, explaining what I saw as I went. Carried within the Light, seeing Creator fold into and out of Themself, moving in Their Way, I arrived at the End. I arrived at the place where all things return to Oneness. I saw, then, that even where all returns to One we are given to live in this moment. I saw that the journey of life is fulfilled in learning to Live. It is Balance. The Spirit spoke and, in the Sacred Silence, said: "Learn to live, take action to improve life, this is The Way."

Nature cannot be tamed, neither can the Spirit be controlled. Freedom is the Spirit's. To think that one may dominate Nature is a great folly. One need not tame the wind to feel its Power, nor must they control the fire to find its warmth. We must learn to work with Nature, to maintain our Balance. One might as well grasp at the wind as though it will remain in their hand to think that they may tame Nature. To seek to control the fire is to be burned. One must learn to tend its flames. It is a dance, this Nature, for She will never give more than She sees fit to give. The ones who seek to dominate Her ways are the ones who will never find peace, for they have pit themself against a force beyond us all.

Our own True Nature cannot be tamed or dominated. We are as the wind and water, the fire and earth where we are within our True Nature. It is then to dance with our own Nature, with Mother Nature. This is the True Nature.

Man, woman, and 2-spirit are equal expressions of Creator. We are all expressions of The Divine.

Within all people The Divine Masculine and The Divine Feminine exist. It is for the same reason that in all things there is negative charge and positive charge energies.

The wisdom, magic, and medicine of indigenous traditions is passed down through its medicine people. This sacred medicine, this sacred work, is often skewed in modern interpretation due to the colonization and christianization of indigenous nations.

An example of this occurrence can be perceived in the use of the word shaman instead of medicine person. Shaman was a word used by anthropologists as they studied a northern Scandinavian indigenous nation. The medicine person of that nation was called a Sa-man. Sa-man means 'one who knows'. The anthropologists decided, then, that all medicine people were Saman even though every nation has their own medicine and their own names for their healers and medicine people.

Much Truth has been skewed by the modern interpretation of indigenous medicine even beyond the word shaman. Every nation has their own medicine and magic, their own wisdom. The medicine people, the wise people and healers, are, and always have been, very sacred people who worked with the Spirit to keep their community.

The medicine people, who the modern world calls 'shaman', could be likened to the mystical practitioners of religious ways of knowing within indigenous traditions. Medicine people, and the ways of medicine and magic, should not be regarded as less than sacred to the utmost degree. The medicine people are, as is said in the modern world, holy people.

The medicine people would pray, and journey in the Spirit to receive Knowledge. Through this work they would be gifted with medicine to heal the people and keep their community.

During colonization it was that the colonizers would first attack the wise people, the medicine people, of a nation. They did this because the medicine people were the keepers of the wisdom and stories of a nation. This pattern continued throughout all of colonization. During the colonization and christianization of indigenous European ways of knowing the medicine people of The Wiccan Way, the witches, were vilified as servants of evil. The druids faced similar persecution during this time. Christian ideology was used to turn the people against their medicine people. During this time witches, the medicine people of The Wiccan Way, would even be burned at the stake for standing in their wisdom. This was called the inquisition, in which all ways of knowing that were not Christian were condemned. The witches were, and still are, as priestesses of the earth. To this day the pentagram, a sacred symbol of consecration in the Wiccan way of knowing, is seen as an evil symbol. Within their community the witch would work the deities and learn the ways of magic in an effort to keep the Balance. The witch also often learned to work with the plant medicines of the land to heal their people. The Wiccan Way is an indigenous tradition and way of wisdom from the northern European region. Theirs is a sacred way and yet witches, even to this day, are vilified for their wisdom. This pattern persisted throughout colonization.

Much of the modern world has a skewed perception of indigenous magic and medicine due to colonization. The use of Christian ideology to vilify indigenous traditions and medicine has left the world without the means to perceive indigenous wisdom accurately.

There are indigenous traditions in all corners of the world. Connecting to the indigenous traditions of where our blood originates from is a great way to reconnect to our Power. Seeking out the traditional plant medicines, the wisdom teachings, or the traditions of our ancestral land is a great way to begin reconnecting to our roots.

The old medicine and magic ways were, and still are, a spiritual science. It was to study the nature of creation through our interconnection with all things. It was, and still is, a precise and Powerful work. The practitioner would train to know the energetic, and through energetic the physical, workings of creation that they may gain insight into how to move Powerfully. The medicine person and/or magical practitioner is also a spiritual scientist.

"Even the mountain is made of the Earth. Were the mountain to no longer be made of Earth it would no longer be a mountain, would it? It would be nothing at all then. It would simply cease to exist."

Even the greatest among us are made of the earth. There is not one who is made great, except that they are the gathering of earth. The one who forgets that humility, who loses their earth, loses their substance. In this loss the fullness of Life leaves them. The 'great' stop being a mountain when they stop being the earth.

My mother told me a story when I was a child. She spoke of a First Nations chief who saw the settlers coming in off their ships. This chief and wise man, having seen the settlers, turned to his people and said: 'These people are mentally ill. They do not know how to live in Balance'.

(Mental illness is now called a pandemic in the modern world)

Mental illness is a cosmic immune system. When we do not honor Mother Earth and the Balance of creation our mind grows sick. This happens because we cannot sustain. When we cannot sustain we become sick and our mind becomes like an enemy.

There is a Nature given to all things that is its Way. This Nature is sacred. It is an expression of Creator. It is the True Nature existing in all things. To be close to Mother Earth and Her ways is also an acknowledgment of this inherent Nature that exists within all things. It is both the acknowledgement of our own journey and the Balance we must keep in our relationship with the world around us.

To seek the Heavens and forget the Earth is much like a tree uprooting itself to reach the light. As one reaches for the treasures of the Heavens their roots must grow deeper into the Earth. If one loses humility and connection they will find that the same light they search for becomes a great wind that carries them away.

Were the tallest redwood to look down upon the other trees of the forest it would turn its gaze from the Light. It would lose sight of its Way. Even the tallest must remember humility. We must all keep our song filled with the spirit of humility.

We are caretakers of the Earth.

To uphold the responsibility that comes with being co-creators reminds the spirit within us of peace. To take care of our environment, including our relationship with humans, is to take care of our own life. To be present with Mother Earth is to also honor our own spirit. When we uphold Balance we create peace in our life.

Sitting on a porch at night, I asked the sapling in front of me: 'how is your night?' The tree said, in a Silent voice, 'I am praising Grandmother Moon'. Looking up into the night sky I saw, then, that Grandmother Moon was full.

A tree spirit could tell you all the secrets of creation if they chose.

There is a great Balance in Nature in which all things are given their place. It is a Great Cycle. The animals, in their life, are also here to nourish us. In a similar way we are here to take care of the Earth and Her children. To honor this great Balance is our responsibility as co-creators. Without our relations, the plants, animals, and elements, there is no life. Without the Balance of keeping our place there can be no life. We are, in Nature, here to take care of our elders, the plants, animals, and elements. We are here to uphold our relations and keep the Balance of this Great Cycle. We are caretakers of the Earth.

There is a great beauty in Nature that humanity perceives when aligned with our natural state. Hidden behind the veils of modern paradigms and the burdens of the past the natural state of humanity perceives this great beauty naturally. This perception is a form of love we innately carry for creation and Mother Earth. We are children of Earth, and so we see Her well when we are well. It is an aspect of our innate interconnection with creation, this unconditional love. As we grow further from our roots we lose sight of the sacredness of Mother Earth. It remains that within every person this love exists.

Consciousness manifests in all planes of creation, expressing as a universal and essential quality of all existence. The elements, plants, and animals are conscious. It is the manifestation of consciousness that changes.

All things have their song. This is the song of the soul, singing in its Way that it may be. It is the song of creation, expressing in all things. The elements, plants, animals, celestial bodies, humans, all things sing their song. In this great symphony called creation the songs of all things come together.

Creation is the dream of Creator. We are all visions within Creator's Infinite dreamscape. This dream is our interconnection, our self-reflection. It is our inner-reality manifesting and interconnecting within a Universal Consciousness. Our own dream is a reflection of Creator's life in us. We exist as trains of Thought in the mind of Creator, expressions of Their Infinite dream.

Altered states are prayer vehicles. They are sacred tools to the same degree as ceremonial tools. Altered states take us to worlds in Spirit and help us see The Way.

One may come to altered states through many ways. One may enter altered states through drumming, chanting, prayer, meditation, ceremony, 'psychoactive' medicines, etc… Even speaking to others in a specific way may cause altered states. Each way of entering an altered state is a sacred vehicle that transports a person to new realms within the Spirit of Creation. When we learn to use the sacred vehicle we enter a sacred tool that helps us walk in the Spirit.

Altered states are very powerful. A person who does not respect the power of altered states will be taken into worlds they are not ready to be in.

Our 'altered state' is shaped by every action and every thing in our life. The one who eats healthy shapes their 'altered state'. The one who eats unhealthy also shapes their 'altered state'. A person who listens to poisonous music infuses their altered state with poison. A person who listens to supportive music infuses their altered state with support. All things are medicine in this way.

There are spirits within the sacred medicines that the modern world calls 'psychedelic' that teach us. They are 'big teachers'. They show us the ways of creation and help us Know Creator. They are very sacred tools with great spirits that live within them.

The big teachers should not be used lightly. They are sacred spirits with Powerful medicine that open the doors of perception. To abuse them can cause great illness. Spiritual injury often looks like mental illness. To abuse a big teacher can cause spiritual injury.

When we use a big teacher the spirit of the sacred medicine takes in the state of our spirit. The spirit of the sacred medicine is imprinted with the realities we take into the medicine. This is one of the reasons indigenous nations have closely guarded their sacred medicines. Their ancestors and the spirit of their people are kept in the memory of the spirit of their sacred medicine.

One may ask the spirit of a big teacher to create a specific space within themself for traditional community. The big teachers love to be known and loved. If asked they will likely to be willing to create a space for traditional community that is separate from the 'modern' spirit. When they do this they build a wall within themself to offer space to those who know their spirit well.

I smoked a sacred medicine, Salvia Divinorum, and was taken into an empty space. Leaving my body I became a gear in that vast emptiness. All else became gears around me, moving together in alignment with each other. Grandmother Salvia showed me, as my gear shifted, that creation moves as a Great Machine shifting in unison. She showed me that one action moves the gears around me that then move the gears around them, continuing out to the ends of creation. I returned to myself after, taking the lesson She taught me as best I could. I continued on understanding that my actions ripple out to the ends of creation and back again in this Great Machine called Life.

Indigenous traditions are much like different flowers growing from the same vine. There is a spirit in each land which is its own, blooming in its Way and shaping its people.

The spirit of Earth is the spirit of Balance

Each land has a spirit which is its own. This spirit is also the memory of its people and its traditions. The ancestors of the land live within Her memory, kept in Her spirit. The traditions of our own ancestors, and all ancestors, live within the memory of the Earth, kept in Her spirit.

There is a Universal Memory that occurs throughout all of creation. The Earth remembers, just as the blood remembers. The realities of creation imprint the substance surrounding us and create a 'universal memory'. This is the memory of the Universal Consciousness. Our own memory reflects this Nature.

I prayed in a sweat lodge. The Grandfathers shone red hot around their edge, darker in their center. As the Cedar was placed on them it burned bright as though eons of the night sky passed before my eyes in a single moment. The stars shone into existence then disappeared, returning to Source.

We are connected to our environment and to the land we live upon intrinsically. It is an innate interconnection that occurs energetically which could be called 'quantum entanglement'. This innate connection means that we, as individuals, are affected by our surroundings energetically whether we acknowledge it or not. It is a kind of resonance within our energetic Nature. We may be affected beyond ways we understand, yet still it remains that we are beings of interconnection. The responsibility we have to Mother Earth is also a responsibility to the spirit of the land we live on. In this, we are also responsible in relation to the indigenous peoples who know the spirit of the land we live on.

Nature is magical and mystical. When we can see the Earth Truly She is a thing filled with much awe and many wonders.

Technology is sacred. It is an expression and expansion of Nature conceived through Knowledge. What is common to this world would have been considered magic in the old world. Technology is sacred, yet so often we forget its value in our lives.

There is a world within the Earth that is the spirit's. Within this world, hidden always on the backs of leaves and between the blades of grass, the spirits of Nature live. There is much magic in that world.

There are spirits that watch over Mother Earth. These are spirits of Nature. They carry with them the energy and memory of a land. They carry with them the energy of their place in creation. For them the old ways never left. These spirits have been known through many ages. They have been a source of great turmoil for those who do not respect Life. They have been guardians to ensure the defeat of the cruel. They have also been a source of great support, wisdom, and joy for those who do respect Life. They are playful beings with much love for those who Know the Earth and respect Life. We share Mother Earth with the spirits of Nature. They are a part of all our relations.

There are many Places of Power across Mother Earth's body. These Natural Temples are sacred sites within Nature that are as homes for Creator. Places of Power, such as Death's Valley, are natural temples. These temples should be regarded with the same reverence as religious temples.

There are energetic currents running through and within Mother Earth. They are known by different names throughout many traditions. These currents are powerful energetic forces. They have been called 'dragon currents', 'ley lines', and other names throughout the history of humanity.

The old ways built many shrines to the spirits of Nature. These shrines, such as fairy mounds, are very sacred. They should be considered as homes to the spirits of Nature within the ways of Earth. All lands have their way of honoring these sacred beings. The spirits of Nature do not take lightly those who do not respect their space. The ones who, even in ignorance, do not adhere to proper respect for these sacred things will find that fate seems to work against them.

There are many possible repercussions a person may incur if they do not show respect to the sacredness of Life and Nature. These repercussions are often the action of spirits who are guardians of Nature. These guardians are very sacred beings who care deeply for Nature.

I was in a conversation with a friend. She told me about the Burning Man festival that took place in Black Rock Desert. Black Rock Desert is a land that still holds the spirit of its indigenous peoples. I said I had never been to a festival. She warned me, as I thought about going, that the desert had flooded during Burning Man the previous year. Once the conversation stopped there was a spirit that approached me in Navajo energy. The spirit, understanding that I can hear, said: "Oy! We hate Burning Man!" I laughed then, understanding that the spirit must Truly be disturbed to travel halfway across the Americas just to tell me that they hate Burning Man.

Desert's, such as Black Rock Desert, are sacred lands. It is likely that the spirits of the area, being disturbed by the festival and what the people were doing on the land, attempted to warn the participants of the festival that they are not welcome there any longer. When the warning was not heeded the spirits of the land warned them further by flooding the desert. This warning is not to be taken lightly. A desert flooding is not a common occurrence. If this warning is not heeded it is likely that further warnings would be given. People have lost their life for not listening to these warnings. We share Mother Earth with the spirits of Nature. Many places across this Earth are as temples in Nature. It is their right, the spirits of the land, to keep their space as they see fit. Just because we have forgotten the sacredness of Life does not mean Life has stopped being sacred. There are many repercussions that occur when we do not respect Nature.

These occurrences are more common than people understand. We often attribute these natural 'warnings' to things out of our control, however the spirits of Nature are very much warning people to respect the land, the life that exists around them, and themselves.

There was a music festival that wanted to put up a permanent stage. In order to put up this stage the festival organizers had to displace an abundance of groundhogs. The organizers killed the groundhogs to put up their stage. During the festival lightning struck. It hit over 100 people.

When we are building homes, seeking resources, wanting to create a gathering, we are also sharing the space we are seeking to use with our relations. We share the space with the plants, animals, elements, and the spirits who live on the land. It is wise that a person should ask the land before using the space they seek to use. Mother Earth is not only ours. We do not know when we are encroaching on sacred sites, seeking to use a space that will not work, or will displace our relations.

All things are made of equality, for All is One. The lives of the plants, animals, and elements are as valuable as our own, and also in their place. It is an Equal Respect.

Those who do not respect the life of the plants, animals, and elements, the sacredness of Places of Power, the original spirit of a land, etc… will find that there are consequences that come to them as though fate has moved against them. It is the Balance of Spirit manifesting. At times it is these sacred spirits watching over Life and warning humans of their folly. Though humanity has forgotten they have not. They hold on that humanity may remember also.

The repercussions of Spirit appear as though fate itself had turned against a person.

Pyramids are ways that traditions would take part in celestial works. They were 'spaceships' that allowed the ones within to journey spiritually within the Heavens and learn the Knowledge found among the stars. The space within the pyramid was considered to be among the stars. The ones who prayed within the pyramid connected to worlds beyond our own.

Pyramids were a way that celestial energy would be brought to the Earth, connecting the Heavens and the Earth. The pyramid would bless the Earth in this way.

Working with plants in a garden bed, I prayed with them. It was not long before one of the little elders spoke to me. The flower showed me that we are One. They said: "you are just me in another life". I saw then that All is One, and that I am just another expression of Nature.

Our ancestors spent thousands of years learning about life and how to live. They developed depth in their ways in a way that the modern world could not possibly achieve. The modern world and the 'modern mentality' has existed for an incredibly short span of time compared to the old ways.

The modern world is rediscovering many things that were well known by our ancestors. Quartz, for instance, was well known to hold energy in a powerful and clear way. In the modern world we use Quartz and refined Quartz, silicon, to hold and move energy in electronic devices. The principles behind Cognitive Behavioral Therapy, the work of challenging thoughts, has also appeared in human history. In Ancient Egypt it is believed that an ancient master practiced Mental Alchemy. Mental Alchemy is the work of transmuting one's mental state from one form to another. It is the work of reshaping our thoughts and our mentality. The modern world is rediscovering many truths that were well known long before 'the modern world'.

In a journey I dived into Earth's center. I saw, in a great and barren temple, a vision of Mother Earth sitting alone on a stone staircase. She was surrounded by people turned to stone. She wept on this staircase, grieving Her children's ways.

Borrowed Earth

The body of I, borrowed from Mother Earth
And from Creator the soul from which I lives
My origin a piece of Their Soul that They have given;
Not a thing do I own, not even I
I have learned
For even my thoughts are borrowed from the Wind

All things are borrowed from Eternity that they may exist
My Truth is a mirror placed before Creator,
My feeling a fluid embrace
My passion a Spirit driven
Living in my borrowed Earth
I see that I belong to that from which I was borrowed from,
And gifted to
That it could never belong to me
This is service, then, that I Live
For Life is built upon the life of many
And each is given to be
In ownership I am lost

That I should give as freely as the trees
And sing my song of praise even as the last of my leaves fall
Every step I take is the step of Mother Earth
Every word spoken is the breath of Creator
Every movement rippling out the the ends of creation
For I am the wind and water, the fire and earth
Borrowed from Eternity

I am the trees in another life,
Having lifted up their roots to walk amongst each other
I am the crow perched outside my window
I Know that one day I will return to Source,
For my I is borrowed,
I will greet Grandfather Death as an old friend,and embrace
Him

Returning what was borrowed, I will fade
The mark I have left on this world a tattoo written upon the flesh of Time and Space,
Forever scrawled in the pages of the Book of Life
The thoughts of those remembering me, borrowed echoes in the cavern of Eternity
I am a prayer of The Divine
A song Mother Earth sings
And every bird's call is as I am,
A note struck in the song of Eternity
For I am, as All is, the wind and water, the fire and earth
Borrowed from the Source of all things

I am the spirit of what can be, the memory of what was
In every cell, from every life I am resonance
I hear it calling me home to an afterlife I was in before this life, and have forgotten
Yet still existing with me, I feel it
Within the borrowed cavern of my Eternity
That Life!

Seeing, within, this journey the hope of a brighter future
Yet to own the future!
This cannot be but a sickness in the minds of those already lost
To take what was borrowed and hold it tight
Until the last drops are squeezed from it,
Life made barren in an attempt to hold against the Truth
That it was never ours
I know also that this is the downfall of humankind
For all is borrowed and nothing can last
Except that it has embraced this No-Thing
We are the wind and water, the fire and earth
We are Borrowed Life, and still Alive
Always Alive
Eternity borrowed from the Eternal
To walk in Borrowed Earth

Spiritual Gifts, Purpose, and Personal Power

Within all people exists a well of infinite willpower. We are the infinite Power of creation manifesting. When we are in alignment with our innate Truth we are most connected to that 'infinite Power of creation' manifesting within and through us. It is our True Nature. It is, then, that our True Nature, our alignment, is an image within us that can overcome all obstacles. Within us all there is a well of infinite willpower. That infinite Power is directly connected to our alignment with our True Nature.

Within us there is a calling. We are called to that which is ours. Our Purpose is made full in that calling. The fullness of that calling is our True Nature, our alignment. To listen to and align with our calling is to walk the path Creator has given us. Our place of Power is directly connected to walking in alignment with our Purpose.

Purpose is not a great thing. Purpose comes from a place beyond greatness.

"Our Purpose is our Power"

The pathway of Purpose is the path our True Nature chooses to walk. This place is the home of our Personal Power.

When we are connected to our True Nature we can hear our Purpose in the calling of our heart.

We may, through our life, hide away our True Nature. When this happens it becomes more difficult to discern our Purpose, our calling, and feel connected to its benefits.

When we carry suffering, it muffles the voice of our calling. It becomes more difficult to discern the True Nature's Way within us. When we, in this place, seek our Purpose and alignment with our True Nature, we connect to the will within us that can overcome all obstacles.

"We are the wind and water, the fire and earth."

Our True Nature is Nature Herself expressing Truth. We are all as the wind and water, the fire and earth where we are True to our Self. We are 'I AM' in this way. We are ceaseless as the Water, humble and Powerful as the Earth, bright as the Fire, and infinite as the Wind. It is Nature that we are so when we are aligned with our Truth

There is an 'anatomy' within the individuality of conscious existence that includes four'forces'. They are: the immediate self, the soulful/hidden self, The Self, and the original design.

Immediate Self

The immediate self is the entirety of who we are in this immediate moment. We are a house our soul has built around itself so that we may live in this world. It is our unconscious state expressing; it is our immediate sense of individuality; it is our joys and our wounds. Our immediate self is often referred to as the 'self'. Our immediate self is ours to create.

The Soulful/Hidden Self

The soulful/hidden self is a part of our immediate connection to our True Nature. Within the spiritual domains of our being, our soulful/hidden self takes the shape of our inner-child and lives within our heart. The clarity of our calling is directly connected to our soulful/hidden self. Within our heart, that calling is a song with an innate character/rhythm. Our soulful/hidden self marks the clarity of that song. The character of that song is called innocence. When our soulful/hidden self is healthy, when our innerr-child is healthy, we are connected to our innocence. When our soulful/hidden self is not healthy, when our inner-child is not healthy, we are not as connected to that innate character, that calling.

The soulful/hidden self has two faces.

The soulful self is our inner-child when our inner-child is healthy and knows Life within us. The soulful self is in good spirits, seeking within the world for Life. They are where our joy is kept. The soulful self is innately called to the fullness of our life. As we grow the character of our soulful self matures. We are the maturing of that seed. Within our heart the soulful self remains, taking the shape of our inner-child within our spiritual domains.

The hidden self is a face of the soulful self that occurs when we have hidden our Truth away from the world. It is a common response to difficult situations and/or to the necessity of assimilation. We forget and hide away our Truth to survive. Through that forgetting we create the hidden self. For those who are spiritually aware, they would perceive their hidden self as their inner-child hiding away or reshaped by their suffering. When our inner-child is not well we walk with a hidden self. When we are with a hidden self we do not have the same connection to our calling, our innocence.

The Self

The Self is who we are in alignment with Natural Law. The Self is our I AM form. The Self has two faces. The two faces of the Self are the pure sense of individuality and the fluid upholding of Life. The two faces of the Self are innately intertwined. It is the I AM form. For those who are spiritually aware, The Self may be perceived within a light in the center of our head. It is our spirit when our spirit is healthy and it is also a song expressing from that center. Our Self marks the fullness of our life. To align with our Self is to step into that which Creator has given us.

The Original Design

Our original design is a 'blueprint' that exists within our unconscious. The blueprint of the original design marks our immediate fullness of being. It is the blueprint of our immediate alignment with our soul's Truth. Within us, our original design operates as a fundamental variable in the process through which our way of being and operating is defined. The nature of our original design is a fundamental variable that defines how we have learned to be and who we are in this immediate moment. The nature of our original design is aligned with the nature of our Self.

Applying the 'anatomy' of our individuality we may perceive important and powerful actions that we can take to work in alignment with the nature of our spirit..

1. Working to heal and help our inner-child is an important part of maintaining our connection with our soul.

2. Our immediate self is something created by us so it is something we may create.

3. That which marks the fullness of our life is alignment with that which is purely ours.

4. To pursue alignment with our pure sense of individuality connects us to the fullness of our life.

5. Our pure sense of individuality is entangled with our will to uphold our place in creation

Our Personal Power is directly connected to how aligned we are with our True Nature. When we are with our soulful self and in alignment with our Self and original design we stand in our Personal Power.

We all have challenges that we are meant to face. We must be brave enough to face these challenges to find the fullness of our life. Our fullness exists where we have had the courage to meet our challenges.

Our challenges teach our soul the lessons it needs as we walk our 'journey of a thousand lifetimes'. To meet our challenges is to walk our soul's journey.

"Within a person's greatest strength exists their greatest weakness"

The one who is confident will easily become blinded by pride; the one who is intelligent will easily become lost in their ideas; the one who is passionate will find distraction comes easy. Our gifts balance themself with weaknesses. Our greatest strength comes also with our greatest weakness. The one who is confident must learn humility; the one who is intelligent must learn to live in this world; the one who is passionate must learn to calm themself and remain directed. True strength comes when we find the will to uphold our weaknesses

"All things have their price"

The soulful choice, the choice of our True Nature, is one that sees the 'weaknesses' of the gifts it will walk with before this life. Our soul knows that each gift carries a 'price' that must be honored. The good hearted one is also often one who doubts themself. All things have their price. It remains that Purpose, being made of the choice of our True Nature, is the path of peace. Within it the soul finds rest. The one whose soulful choice chooses service may carry that which others do not have to bear. It remains that they will find their rest in alignment with their Purpose. This one may bear the weight of much they feel they haven't chosen. Their soul has chosen that which is theirs. All things have a 'price'. Balance is The Way.

"Our Purpose is a choice our soul has chosen even before this life."

"The humility to admit one's weakness is one of the greatest of strengths"

"To be empowered in 'weakness' is to know True Strength"

To be empowered in our weakness heals the spirit, the being, that it may be fulfilled in its Way. True strength is not the absence of weakness. True strength is the will to understand and uphold our weaknesses. True strength is the will to stand in Balance and be empowered in our 'weakness'. The one who is good hearted is likely to be doubtful of themself. It is for the Power of their good heart that they have learned to think in a way that doubts themself. What we perceive as weakness is Truly an aspect of our strength. To find our Power in our 'weakness' is to cross a bridge towards True Empowerment. The one who seeks confidence must be willing to find their Power in the place of self-doubt. The one who is innately confident must be willing to find their Power in acknowledging where they are wrong, that pride may not blind them to their Way. Through finding their Power in the 'weakness' of their gifts they will find a path to True Empowerment.

Those who walk in their Purpose must also adhere to wisdom, unity, and responsibility in the search for fullness. The way of the Spirit, which is of Purpose, is fulfilled in Balance. A choice made without understanding responsibility, wisdom, and the Life that is around us cannot uphold the Nature of Spirit. It is wise, then, to ask: 'what is my soulful choice made with wisdom?'

We are all given to keep spiritual gifts.

Spiritual gifts are the medicine of our True Nature, our alignment, expressing into our immediate way of being. The one who is gifted to speak has a True Nature aligned with speech. The one who is gifted to feel, such as an empath, has a True Nature aligned with feeling. The one who is gifted to walk between the worlds has a True Nature that is called to Spirit. A spiritual gift is the medicine of our True Nature expressing into our life.

Spiritual gifts are an expression of the True Nature existing in all things. Every thing in existence is given to carry spiritual gifts. It is the medicine of the True Nature expressed into life. Cedar's gift, for instance, is cleansing. The spiritual, or energetic, gift of Cedar is cleansing.

Spiritual gifts are ways of being that we are given to be. Our True Nature expresses through us and reflects the innate qualities of our spirit, our individuality. A spiritual gift is a way of being that we are naturally called to be.

Each spiritual gift we are given aligns with our Purpose in this life. These 'gifts' are expressions of our soul and guide our Way.

A spiritual gift is not, generally, an innate skill, rather it is a calling. It is not that one who is gifted to speak is innately skillful at speaking. It is that their innermost nature as an individual aligns with speech. It is in a similar way that an empath's True Nature aligns with feeling the world around them. It is through the work of learning to uphold our spiritual gifts that they become blessings and rare skills.

A spiritual gift can be both a blessing and a curse. It is through honoring Balance and upholding our True Nature that a spiritual gift becomes a blessing and a rare skill.

The potential blessing of a spiritual gift is equal to the potential for it to cause suffering. The Power of a spiritual gift is like any Power. Its potential is both for expansion and destruction.

Should a person align with their Purpose, learning to uphold their spiritual gifts, they will find both Personal Power and peace.

The 'mental illnesses' of the modern world are, at times, products of spiritual gifts that a person has not learned to keep.

Our spiritual gifts are aspects of our energetic nature. When we do not uphold the balance our body requires physical illness forms. It is in a similar way that when we do not uphold our energetic nature, energetic illness forms.

'Each spiritual gift carries with it, in equal measure to its Power, a burden, a lesson, and a consequence.'

There is a burden, lesson, and consequence that accompanies every spiritual gift. When the burden and lesson are not upheld the spiritual gift becomes imbalanced for its presence. This creates illness. The more Powerful the gift, the greater its burden. The more Powerful the blessing of the gift's fullness the more it demands of a person. When we learn to honor the burden and lesson of our gifts, which is to uphold their nature in us, the gift becomes a blessing and a rare skill. When we do not uphold our spiritual gifts there is a consequence that forms within us naturally.

The burden of a spiritual gift is a weight that we must learn to bear. The greater the gift the greater the will of its keeper must be. It is the True Nature that overcomes all obstacles. The one who is gifted to speak will find that speech comes easy, yet if they are not careful of their words they will speak their own destruction. The one who is gifted to walk between the worlds must learn to keep a strong spiritual and physical foundation or they will become lost between them. To honor the burden of a spiritual gift is to learn the discipline that is necessary to carry its weight with responsibility and wisdom.

The lesson of a spiritual gift is the teachings that surround the upholding of its burden. The one who is gifted to speak must learn to keep their Balance, to take the time they need for themself. Through their learning they will find the pathway to the rare skill that their gift has the potential of being. The one who is an empath must learn to be consistent in response to emotions and to discern the emotions that are their own. To learn the lessons of a gift is to walk the pathway of fulfilling our Purpose. It is also the pathway of learning to bear its burden.

The consequence of a spiritual gift is the byproduct of not upholding its burden and lesson. When the one who is called to walk between the worlds does not uphold their gift they become lost between the worlds. The one who speaks will speak their destruction. The one who feels will lose their Self in that ocean. The one who thinks will be drawn deep into their thoughts. There is an equal consequence for not upholding our True Nature's gifts.

Integrity is a superpower.

All are given, to differing degrees, spiritual gifts. There are those who carry more and there are those who carry less. The one who carries more is, in traditional ways of knowing, considered to be one who is blessed. Creator gave them much to bear and so they are one who, in wisdom and fullness, will stand with much to offer.

The place where we are aligned with our soul's Truth is a place where we find the Sacred Silence naturally. It will be much easier for a person to find the Sacred Silence within that which they are called to than to find it in places they force themself to be.

To know our Self is also to understand where we find our Purpose. This place can be anything and it is always a calling. The one who finds their peace performing and making music is walking the same journey as the one who finds their peace in prayer and the study of Spirit. The one who feels peace working on cars is called to work on cars. They will find Creator where they have walked this journey. The one who is called to medicine and healing will find Creator where they have walked this journey. One is not greater than another, rather All is One in Eternity. Through this we may see that Life itself is The Way.

Peace comes from maintaining a healthy lifestyle in all aspects of one's life. This work, of creating health, becomes clearer and easier when we walk a path aligned with our Purpose.

As we walk in alignment with our True Nature we are naturally urged towards Balance and health. Our True Nature strengthens our resolve when we honor our Way. The work of creating a blessing of our gifts is also the natural urge to 'return to balance'. This work is often more about releasing suffering than overcoming willfully.

As we grow within our Way our way of knowing grows, becoming an expression of Self that is our knowing.

As one continues in their work they develop their knowing. Their inner calling becomes a skill regarding their calling as they continue in the Way of their True Nature. This becomes their knowing.

Consistency in response to experience, gained through detached observation and focused on achieving peace and balance, is a powerful action in manifesting the blessings of the gifts we are given to be. It is responsibility.

The one who seeks their True Nature will find what works for them. It is to become the Truth that exists within that we seek what works for us. The one who does not find help in meditation may need to find another way to connect to the Sacred Silence. The one who does not feel connected to prayer may need to find another way to cultivate their spirit.. What works for us is an expression of our Purpose. It is more important that we turn to what works for us than that we persist in a thing that does not work for the sake of it being given to us.

To become disciplined is to learn why we choose to act. To find discipline is to let go of the suffering that compels us into places of stagnancy and to deeply understand why we seek what we seek. In Eternity, in 'Heaven', a person would not seek to be idle. They would, rather, seek to act in a way that fulfills them. Discipline comes from understanding that state of being that exists within us. The one who is completely healthy is innately driven toward the discipline that knows Life. What would you choose as your work in Eternity? To answer this question is to find the seed of discipline. To become the answer is to find freedom.

The fullness of our Power exists behind our suffering and hidden pains. To Know our Purpose and uphold our spiritual gifts is also to walk our healing journey.

A healing journey often asks us to participate in trauma recovery, change core beliefs, learn to apply processes that maintain balance, develop self-awareness, etc… A healing journey is about letting go of the things that keep us in imbalance and stepping into the things that keep our Balance. It is a journey that we walk slowly, step by step, guided by our True Nature.

The state of Personal Power is to learn to be as the wind and water, the fire and earth. It is to stand in the True Nature.

The work of learning integrates wisdom. As we live we experience. Through experience we develop a clearer sense of how creation operates and how we may relate skillfully to creation's operation. Observation and the ability to process information is a great power that is available to all people always. As long as we continue learning we will remain on a journey that leads to peace. Not a thing, having come to Know, chooses its own dis-ease and destruction. To persist in learning, then, is to overcome suffering.

When a person is living in their Personal Power the spiritual gifts of their True Nature are upheld and applied and their Purpose is fulfilled. Personal Power is not without the upholding of our gifts and the honoring of our Purpose.

To honor our own Purpose, our Truth, becomes the capacity to honor the Truth of all things. The one who has not honored their Purpose will find that they struggle to honor the Life that exists around them. Everything is conceived with Purpose. To not honor Purpose is to not honor the nature of our existence. To not honor the True Nature of our existence becomes poison in the unconscious.

Spiritual Power and Personal Power are powers that dance. They are not powers that control. The one who lives in Personal Power dances the dance of their True Nature. The one with Spiritual Power dances with the Spirit of Creation, moving in Their steps. True Power is not control. It is 'self-mastery'.

Life is a practice which we may become skillful regarding. The one who is skillful ably responds to their environment, both internal and external.

Have faith in the journey of your Purpose. To burden one-self without wisdom leads into dis-ease.

It is through True Knowledge that potential expands.

The state of True wellness is that we have learned to Live.

All things are conceived of Truth and with Purpose. The Balance of Life is fulfilled in our own fulfillment. All is One.

The Fundamental Gifts

Through understanding these fundamental gifts we may come to understand the nature of spiritual gifts with greater clarity. Through understanding the nature of spiritual gifts we may come to discern our own.

The Speaker

The Speaker feels a natural urge to speak and to be in community with others. The speaker is often very confident, for their gift demands it of them. The Speaker is naturally drawn towards speech. It is for this reason they become proficient with speech.

The Speaker can become lost in community. They can lose connection with their substance for the sake of their urge to speak. Their confidence can blind them to The Way. It is a natural by-product of the gift of The Speaker that a person may lose track of their Way within speech.

A Speaker would do well to have a practice of self-awareness. They would do well to find a space for themself and for their thoughts. They would be wise to exercise their ability to be aware of when they need such a space. Through this they may develop the mechanisms that help them turn their gift into a blessing.

The Thinker

The Thinker is gifted to think. Their mind is called towards thought. They are naturally more drawn to developing insight. They are often inward drawn for this reason. The Thinker is called to thought so they spend more time in their thoughts.

The Thinker can become lost in their thoughts and forget the world around them. They can lose their connection with the world around them due to their natural inward draw. They may become distant from the world for the sake of their gift. Through this they may lose their fullness.

The Thinker would do well to be present with their presence in the world around them. The Thinker may need to be more conscious of maintaining or creating healthy relationships, including friendships. They may need to push themself to spend time around others. Through this they may turn their gift into a blessing.

The Hunter

The Hunter is strong within the process of their mind that is focus and awareness. Having strength in this part of their being can make The Hunter easily distracted when not genuinely interested. This gift, however, also creates a strong capacity for focus when a person is genuinely interested. The Hunter can be easily distracted and can also 'tunnel-vision' when genuinely interested. Strength in the process of focus and awareness creates a greater capacity in both focus and awareness..

The Hunter's gift is easily distracted when without genuine interest in an activity. When without a viable focal point that accesses their capacity for focus for a long period of time, The Hunter can become less able to access their capacity for focus. Over time, and if they do not find a focal point, their capacity for focus may diminish.

The one with the gift of The Hunter would do well to find a focal point that they 'tunnel-vision' with. They tunnel vision because there is genuine interest within their spirit regarding the activity. When they have found this focal point they may learn to 'hone their mind' on other activities by bridging the focus or by deeply understanding the value of the action to their own wellbeing. Through this their gift may become a blessing.

The Empath

The empath is naturally attuned to the energetic and emottional resonance of their surroundings. They are naturally attuned to the emotional frequency of those around them. Around a person who is angry they may begin to feel angry. Around a person who is sad they may begin to feel sad. This gift makes an empath a great healer, however there are various difficulties that may arise. The empath is naturally more attuned to the resonance of the world around them.

The empath may become lost in the resonance of the world around them. They may become lose themself in the Ocean. If the empath is not able to discern and work with their own emotions well they become scattered and lose the ability to maintain emotional consistency. It is more likely for an empath to lose emotional stability than it is for those who do not have the gift of The Empath.

The empath must learn to work with emotion well and discern the emotions that are theirs from those that are not. It is a good idea for an empath to ask: 'is this mine?' when they feel an emotion that may not be theirs. The empath must learn to observe their emotions and learn to work with their own emotions responsibly. If they do not learn to observe and work with their emotions, developing good mechanisms, they will likely find that they become lost in the resonance of the world around them. Through this The Empath turns their gift into a blessing.

The Good Hearted One

The good hearted one is blessed with the will to do good in the world around them. They naturally think more of the world around them so operate in a way that is present with the world around them. We all have a good heart within us, however the good hearted one is more attuned to the natural instinct of doing good in the world.

The good hearted one, for the sake of being blessed to think of the world, may become doubtful of themself and give heedlessly. They may find that the nature of their internal way of thought makes them doubtful. They will likely contemplate the perceived wellbeing of others more than their own wellbeing. They may find themself giving heedlessly for the sake of making others feel comfortable. The good hearted one, for the sake of thinking of the world, may give too freely and become doubtful. When the good hearted one has taken on self-doubt they lose the blessing of their good heart. When they have given too freely of themself they become resentful in their unconscious and lose the blessing of their good heart.

The good hearted one would do well to learn to stand in their Personal Power. The good hearted one who learns to keep their gift is Truly blessed, for everywhere they go they are welcome. When the good hearted one learns to stand in their Personal Power they step into a place of fullness. All doors open to the good hearted one who knows the blessing of their gift.

The Spirit Walker

The Spirit Walker naturally moves through the veils that hide the worlds of Spirit. Theirs is a Powerful gift so it is met with a great weight. The spirit walker perceives the unseen naturally so it is necessary that they create and uphold a foundation that can sustain seeing the unseen.

The spirit walker, for the sake of their natural capacity, experiences the realities of a spirit walk. Their Personal Illusion reflects upon their mind naturally. This can easily delude those without the poise to understand what is and what isn't. A person, to sustain a spirit walk, must pass through their Personal Illusion through discerning Truth. If they do not, their Personal Illusion sits between them and Spirit, defining their reality. Their reality becomes that which they believe. A spirit walker without the foundation to sustain their natural capacity enters into the realities that exist within their unconscious. These realities, then, may draw them in, creating a 'separate reality' that does not uphold the Spirit. At this point a spirit walker may become very ill and lose themself between the worlds. A person who has lost themself as a Spirit Walker is often called, in western medicine, schizophrenic.

The gift of The Spirit Walker is great so there is much work that must be done to keep it. The spirit walker must learn to discern innate Truth through their Personal Illusion. They must create integrative foundation for their True Nature, their Self. They must seek out traditional wisdom and create spiritual routine. They mustt walk their healing journey and reconcile. A person who has already entered into delusion may need to gain substance by directing their mind solely to the substantial Truths in their environment. Anything that is not tangible must be turned away for the one who has already entered into delusion. Through these actions a person may come to sustain the gift of the spirit walker.

To learn more about the gift of The Spirit Walker and the work required to sustain it see the section: Magic, Energy, and The Spirit World

Grief

The spirits spoke
As I saw
A person numbed, emptied by the world
Advertised in their grief that others may pay to speak their sorrows
They said, the good spirits,
We grieve the Earth, within
For the emptiness of our hearts
The illness of our minds
Is also our spirit grieving our connection with our Mother
You cannot feel the Life within the concrete
Nor can you be filled by an empty world
Our fullness is made of a thing we have forgotten
Even to have forgotten that we lost it

The Heavens and the Earth are One
People seeking the Spirit, forgetting the Earth
Gazing into the sun as though it will bring them peace; that it may make them whole
People seeking the Earth, forgetting Her spirit
Accumulating wealth to fill a void that material can never satisfy
Depressed, swinging from side to side
Made sick by beliefs, in sickness made
To fix what was never broken, but forgotten
And even stolen from those who knew it well

The children of a new age, processed and forgotten
We grieve our loss in ways we cannot recognize
An illness made of a Truth beyond the understanding of industry
Fame will not bring joy
Neither will wealth satisfy that Silent, Little Voice
So diagnose, without compromise
Tell us we are wrong for being

And we will believe this thing as it is spoken
Becoming sick for its saying,
We will continue
In that darkness we will continue until we can no longer
The grief remains

Hurt is not an endless void
Nor that grief without its movement
That loss is not infinitely insatiable
That illness, not without peace
We grieve a connection we forgot we had
Then advertised in our grief,
The sign saying let me fix you for 50 dollars an hour
Until the bank is as empty as the spirit
Our system collapses,
Into ruin
That we may be renewed again
That we may remember

The Earth will reclaim Her children
As She reclaims a world grieving Her loss
For we are lost, grieving Her
And dead for our ways
We say, amongst the lost souls,
That our way is death and sickness is forever
That there can be no peace in life
Except among the enlightened few
All is made of Truth
The Heavens and the Earth are One
We have lost them both
The grief remains

We feed our void with the sorrows of others
Without realizing we are feeding a void filled with sorrow
Buried beneath the gathering burdens of industry and expansion,

We continue in our loss
A sickness we forgot we even carried
Still, who can blame those who don't know for not knowing
When even the source of ignorance has been forgotten?

"Do unto others as you would have done unto yourself, and unto yourself do the same"

"Attachment is the origin of conflict"

"Our inner world becomes our external environment"

Society, Community, and Relationships

"Do unto all else as you would have done unto yourself, and unto yourself do the same"

For more see the section: *Living - The Golden Rules*

"Seek first the peace within, knowing that inner-peace is also the peace of the world."

We are not separate from the world. In Unity we are One with the world around us. The one who does not seek their own peace does not feel well enough to keep peace with others. The one who does not keep peace with others, likewise, cannot fulfill their own peace. The soul, who is the keeper of our peace, is not separate from the world. Our own peace is also the peace we bring into the world. It is, then, that one should seek first their own peace, knowing that that fullness is where they become one who keeps peace. To seek our peace, being an internal work, is to become able to maintain Balance with all our relations.

"Our inner-world becomes our external environment"

The state of our inner-world becomes the state of our life. That which exists within us impacts how our unconscious operates, changing how we relate to our external environment. That which exists within our unconscious, also, attracts or repels within the energetic domains of creation, changing our external environment. Through this our internal state becomes our external environment.

"One cannot compromise on their Self without losing peace."

Boundaries are a way that our spirit structures our existence in the vastness of creation. We are defined more by what we choose to not be than by what we choose to be. A person cannot compromise on their Self without losing their potential for peace. The loss of that potential, then, becomes the loss of our ability to uphold our place in creation and in community. The Self is who we are in alignment with Natural Law. It is our pure sense of individuality and the fluid upholding of Life.

"We are all the coming together of many things."

All people are the amalgamation of many things. Experiences, beliefs, soulful nature, ancestry, knowledge, community, emotions, health, society, spirit, traumas and burdens, joys and passions, etc… Life is vast and confusing, yet we remain the coming together of many things. It is through all that we are that we are made. Living can be a vast and overwhelming reality at times. It remains that we are all drops of water in an ocean, seeking to make sense of it all.

"The shape of reality begins within."

The reality we experience is defined by our unconscious state. Those who are not able to observe their experience in a detached way have their experience decide their reality more so than the Truth itself. The shape of reality is a personal invention. The question, then, is: 'what is my Self's?'

"Attachment is the origin of conflict."

Were two people without the ability to detach from their viewpoints to discuss a topic, even with similar viewpoints, then the first inconsistency in their beliefs would spark an argument. If they continued without the detachment required to observe and find peace with each other this small inconsistency could end a relationship. Nobody is always right, nor does 'right' matter more than peace. Attachment is the origin of conflict.

"Choice is a face of Creator"

The way we are given to choose is a face of Creator. We each come into this world with a calling, a Purpose. When we can remember that choice, made soulfully and with wisdom, is both beyond us and our own it becomes easier to understand how to uphold Life.

"Individuality is a universal quality of creation"

All people are different from each other to some extent. Not a single person is an exact reflection of another. The binding constructs of creation make it so individuality is a universal quality of existence. Though there are similar qualities that appear in many, individuality remains a universal constant. The one who cannot come to peace with difference, then, will never find their peace. In the inability to acknowledge the sacredness of difference much is lost. Difference is a face of The Divine.

To understand the emotions of others is to give compassion to our own; to not give compassion to our own is to create room to misunderstand the emotions of others.

"To be consistent in response to emotions is the heart of emotional wellbeing."

Emotions are the savor and vibrancy of life. Emotional wellbeing occurs as we respond to emotions with ability and consistency. To learn to be consistent in response to one's emotions creates emotional wellbeing. Through responding ably to emotions we retrieve the vibrancy and savor of life.

There are two types of emotions, they are: expansive and fundamental/constrictive.

Expansive emotions include joy and love. They are emotions that expand our state of being and remind us of the beauty of life. Joy is an energetic surge that happens in relation to beautiful experiences. Love is an energetic surge that happens in relation to connection.

Fundamental/Constrictive emotions include anger and sadness. They are emotions that help us return to Balance after difficult experiences. Anger is an energetic push against injustice. It is upheld best when its energy is applied to create the Balance that was lost. Sadness is an energetic push to cleanse emotional pain. It is upheld best when it is able to move the energetic pain that it has responded to.

All emotion is valid. There is a deeper logic, a reasoning, that occurs within our inner-nature that makes us feel. It is because of this deeper logic that emotion is valid. It occurs in recognition of a deeper logic. Even if an emotion does not feel 'right', that does not mean that our innocence has not learned to be what feels this way. When we honor the validity of emotions we may come to a place of responding to them well. This, then, helps us retrieve our emotional wellbeing.

"Emotion teaches us of who we are"

How we feel teaches us of our True Nature. When we are consistent in relation to our emotions we come to understand our True Nature in more profound ways. When our emotions are unwell it is more difficult to discern our True Nature within them.

Emotion is a constant in life.

"The one who sustains through destruction is ill."

The need to hate; the urge to put others down; the addiction; etc... is a sign of imbalance within one's inner-nature. The one who sustains through destruction is ill. The illness causes the unconscious to sustain its dis-ease through destruction. Destruction, of both self and the world, becomes the sustenance of the illness, the poison. One who lives in imbalance is one who has lost their ability to sustain. It is suffering.

"We are in a relationship with all of creation. We relate to all aspects of our environment, therefore we are in a relationship with all things."

Our relationship is not only with other humans, nor is our ability to uphold our relationships solely dependent upon our ability to relate to humans. We are also in a relationship with the animals, plants, and elements. When we can respect them it becomes much easier to respect humans.

“We come to know our Self through our connection to the world.”

The way we relate to the world around us defines who we are at an unconscious level. Without upholding our relationship with the world around us we become lost, for it is through our interconnection that we come to know ourself. All is One.

“To respect the world around us is to respect Creator”

Respect all things, for in all things lives the heart of Creator. The one who respects Life respects Them; the one who does not respect Life disrespects Them. They live in all things, even that which is seemingly opposed.

To learn to respect all things is a work of becoming. It is often not something we innately know, for the body does not automatically know the spirit. This becoming is gained as we see the Truth beyond and within us. As we become this Truth, so to do we find that respect was always within us to give.

“Our Self exists where we have learned to keep Balance with all our relations“

As we feel within we act around us even when we cannot recognize how we are Truly feeling. Our ability to sustain supportive relationships is a direct product of our own inner-work.

Observing the way we behave is a way to discern what we are enduring within.

The ones who seek to help should first achieve their own fullness.

The willingness to accept and honor other ways of knowing and being is the foundation through which society may come to sustain. The ones who cannot find peace with difference are the destruction of community. Truly, difference is one of the great beauties of the Spirit. Truth is not ours to decide. It is ours to respect and honor for all peoples and ways of knowing, remembering, also, that Balance is The Way.

Supportive and sustainable community is one of the main forces that made humans human. It is when we could come together that we became human.

A leader was once a steward of community. The idea of politics and hierarchy began when the one who held the position of leader decided they were entitled to it.

A society is the sum of the mentality of its people regardless of who retains power. The power of the leader is that they may shape the mentality of their people and the image of their culture.

Those who seek change, the revolutionaries, must first 'revolutionize' themself. True revolution begins within. True change is an internal transformation. It is a reconditioning within which the individual sheds, completely, the 'enslaved mind', stepping into fullness. To condition oneself is a natural occurrence. The True change of the revolutionary is the surpassing of the conditioning of the world within. It is through the surpassing of 'self' that the world changes as a whole. We must become the change we seek in the world. The revolutionary must first revolutionize their own world. It is through this 'self-revolution' that True change becomes possible.

This work is also the work of healing.

"Those who cannot see the Truth of the world they live in will not find their Self."

There are great tragedies in the world that many have learned to overlook and ignore. The one who does not acknowledge the reality of suffering cannot see their Way. It is for the reason that they have chosen blindness that they are blind.

On Turtle Island there has been great tragedies, yet much of the modern North American culture cannot see past its ways. Genocide, cultural genocide, slavery, theft of land, etc... cannot be disregarded without creating mental illness. It remains that many see only the material treasures of a modern world that is slowly killing itself. They do not see the suffering upon which the North American culture is built. The justification of suffering is universal. To acknowledge the reality of suffering, without justification, is to open one's eyes to peace. The one who cannot acknowledge Truth will not be able to uphold Balance because they have already turned away from the essence of Balance. That one may abide suffering is suffering itself.

In the Vietnam war 1,000,000 Vietnamese people were killed, including women and children. The country had a population of approximately 22 million people at the time. There were 50,000 American casualties in a country with a population of approximately 200 million. All life is sacred, not only the life we are told to see. The Self is not blind.

The tragedies of our world cannot be disregarded without feeding into the cycle of destruction and illness. The path to peace and fullness is reconciliation. The effect of tragedy on the people who endure carries on generationally. Cruelty, also, kills the soul of the abusers and, within the subtle domains of creation, creates consequence that passes on generationally. The one who justifies suffering becomes suffering.

The Self is not blind to Truth, nor does it see only as it is told to. The justification of suffering is universal.

Unconditional Love is a universal energetic force.. It is the 'glue' of creation, binding and connecting all things. To Love, in love's Truth, is to learn to be without condition and without compromise.

One of the greatest things we can give is Unconditional Love.

To love one's self unconditionally is a gate into the Self.

We are all given our place in this world. The warrior who stands for Balance without the pacifist who speaks will find that one arm of their stand is lost. The pacifist without the warrior will also lose much. We are all given a place in this world. It is marked by our Purpose, our True Nature. In wisdom and in the pursuit of peace one is not greater than another for being. The student who learns to heal without the farmer who grows food will find little sustenance in their learning; the farmer will likewise find less fullness in their life. The scientist who invents without the tradesperson who builds will find that their ideas are emptied of meaning; the tradesperson will have less for the absence of the scientist also. We must honor and respect all places within this great work, for all are given their place even before this life. All is One.

"Suffering is the root of all evil."

When we carry suffering we become altered by it. Suffering alters our unconscious, creating a potential for evil. It is much like when a person is hungry they may become angry. A person with suffering is always agitated in a way that alters how they think. When this alteration becomes severe evil occurs.

Suffering is the destroyer of worlds

It has been said that money is the root of all evil, however money is a tool that has offered many opportunities that could not exist without it. As with all tools, it is the hands of the one who wields it that decides whether it sustains or destroys. Power without wisdom is destruction. Money is not the root of all evil, rather it is that we participate in the suffering that causes evil. The rich man is surely able to give should they know their giving as a thing valuable above wealth. Money is a tool that we must be wise enough to use. The one who invents could not invent without a system that allows them to have food, shelter, water, etc… while also inventing. It is not money that caused the schisms that separated our world into broken sections. It is that our world is suffering and built upon suffering.

Power without wisdom is destruction. The modern powers, the systems that have allowed us to exist in new ways, such as money and technology, are tools. When we do not honor the power of a tool it becomes our destruction. To honor the Power of a thing becomes the wisdom of Unity.

Power is a sacred tool with two faces. They are wisdom and force. The one who holds power carries a sacred tool through which they may shape the world around them. To carry power is a responsibility.

Power's first face is wisdom. When power is upheld in pursuit of Balance it is called wisdom. The one who keeps power well knows the wisdom of the power they keep.

Power's second face is force. Force could also be called potential for expansion. The one with power gains force. They gain greater potential to shape the world around them. The force of power cannot go without notice. The force of power demands wisdom or its expansive potential becomes destructive.

Within The Way, the rich must give as their peace demands; the poor must rise as their peace demands; the powerful must humble themself; the weak must strive to know their strength; the broken must heal; the full must stand; the lost must find; the teachers must know their ignorance; the warriors must honor their weakness. Balance is The Way.

Technology is sacred.

It is when we stop holding Life sacred that we become our own destruction.

The fundamental equations of creation determine that expansion without foundation leads into collapse. When expansion, which is force, occurs without the wisdom to keep it there is no foundation that allows the expansion of energy. In this, it is predetermined at a physical level to collapse its 'system'. This 'collapsing' of energy is a great source of suffering for many. When power does not uphold its innate force it becomes blind to its impact. When force is not held with proper wisdom it becomes destruction. When the Balance of Power is not kept the sacred tool turns inward. When the force turns inward it takes much from both its carrier and the ones within their power's reach.

When one with power, who has not kept Balance, reaches out into the world they may sustain themself until there is nothing left to consume. The collapsing energy seeks a way of sustaining its destructive potential. It, then, consumes what is within its reach and creates suffering in its wake. It is an energetic pattern. Eventually power without Balance will collapse. It is Natural Law.

Disempowerment is a great societal ill that has pervaded many social systems. The powerful, in order to retain power, disempower the masses. When a person is disempowered they naturally act in destructive ways. A person who is disempowered is not capable of mental health. That which cannot be full within itself has already begun to destroy itself. That which destroys itself seeks to consume of the world to sustain its self-destruction. Empowerment is an aspect of peace. A society built upon the shoulders of the disempowered will one day consume itself and collapse.

Without equality, and equity in pursuit of equality, as fundamental principles a society is only biding its time until collapse.

When a society allows inequality to exist within its paradigm it creates two expressions of division. These expressions of division are the loss of the principles that sustain Balance. This loss, then, precedes the collapse of a system.

Those who are 'above' is the first expression of inequality within a social system. The keeping of Balance is a mentality. The one who expects to be above operates mentally in a way that needs external forces to sustain. This mentality is, then, a mentality of consumption. The division that expects to be above is itself based in suffering. It is for this reason that to expect to be 'above' creates suffering. That suffering, being energetic sickness, must consume to sustain itself, for it has forfeited its fullness.

Those who are put 'below' is the second expression of inequality within a social system. The ones put below must either rise up or remain in a way that is disempowered. In order to keep their peace they must stand against the imbalance and injustice. If they allow disempowerment to defeat them then they can longer keep Balance. They must, within that loss, consume to sustain. It is division. This division then prepares a system for collapse or revolt.

The expressions of division within a social system apply strongly to leadership. The leader cannot stand above the rest, nor can they keep a mentality of one who does while a society flourishes.

During the time when inequality exists within a social system its paradigm will be one of consumption, distraction, and division. This is an expression of a Natural Law, being a physical expression of a universal, energetic, Nature.

Universal Principle sustains. The universe has yet to implode. Universal Principle is the heart of sustenance. To create a system that is not aligned with Universal Principle, which is Natural Law, can never sustain.

To create a social system that does not align with the natural state of existing as humans is much like building a vehicle that cannot fit a person. When a society does not honor the realities of existing as humans; bodily, mentally, emotionally, spiritually, soulfully, relatively, etc… it is a vehicle designed to fail in its purpose.

Change is a constant. Change is a Universal Principle. A system that cannot adapt as is wise will seed its collapse. Attachment to a single idea binds a system to a lack of adaptability. A system must be designed in the idea that all things change as they proceed through time. Regardless of the degree of change that is wise, it remains that to attach to the structure of a social system does not align with Natural Law.

Fundamental actions take precedence over expansive actions. To understand the nature of living is more important for sustainability than knowledge itself. It is in a similar way that learning to learn is more important than learning itself. The one who comes to know yet never understands how to live is given a power they are never taught to maintain. The one who is made to learn, yet does not understand how to, is offered an opportunity they do not know how to take advantage of. Fundamental actions take precedence over expansive actions. It is easy to forget that we must learn to keep a strong foundation before building on top of it.

The best a society can do is create the optimal environment for the success of its citizens. A society that assumes control over its people divides them.

A society is a living organism much like the human body.

To understand the reason why an action is important at an unconscious level helps to build the will to act. Our mind operates in accordance with our unconscious drive. When a person does not understand the value of a thing well, both to themself and their life, they won't feel driven to it. At times we must teach first why a thing is important so that it is understood at an unconscious level. This principle applies strongly to individuality, being that a person will be more driven to act within their Purpose. When a person doesn't understand the significance of what they are doing and how it can improve their life they do not have the same capacity for motivation.

Suffering takes away from the capacity of unconscious drive. The one who carries suffering, even if they are not consciously aware of it, has that suffering weigh down upon their capacity for motivation. Their unconscious ability to create drive is dampened.

The children are the future and every child matters. It is well known that few children break a cycle that they are taught at an early age, yet still we teach fear conditioning, self-denial, 'consumption to sustain', skewed histories, etc…

The one who is heard is the one who is ready to listen. It is the nature of the spirit that the one who does not feel heard will not listen unless they disempower their spirit to do so. We must honor and acknowledge all voices in the circle, for each is given its medicine and its Way. The greatest of wisdoms may appear from the mouth of the child. The one who cannot hear Their/their voice, even from the smallest places, cannot Know their/Their Way.

To create room for imbalance is to step into illness.

The freedom of the mind is a great Power. We are all capable of changing the world.

A social system that feeds the power hungry, that offers power to those who seek it, has given over to those who do not deserve power. The ones who Know The Way often do not seek power. A leader must be willing to humble themself. The one who does not humble themself is, in the nature of the mind, attached to the idea of power. This attachment will become, in one way or another, an imbalance that expresses into the actions of the leader. The social system that feeds the ones who seek power has prepared the system for collapse.

Sacred Silence, being the meditative mind, is a powerful tool for maintaining a healthy life-style. It is for the same reason that Sacred Silence is an important aspect of maintaining a healthy community and society.

Linear thought cannot see beyond its own preconception for the same reason that tunnel vision does not see beyond its tunnel. Linear thought is better applied as a tool. It is detachment, the will to take a step back and see, which finds the fullness of The Way. This way of thought is 'spiralist thought' or integrative thought. It is well achieved through the study of wisdom.

The way of thought that seeks to overcome Nature cannot Live fully. We must seek to align with the Natural Way and return to our Nature.

The schism in our societies, our modern way of thought, is a dissonance relating to the Natural way..

When the linear way of thought becomes the only socially acceptable way of thought it is innate that a society pits itself against the Natural Way.

It is natural that humanity seeks The Way. It is when we become distant from our True Nature that we stop seeking The Way.

Those who have forgotten often respond to those who stand in their Power in destructive ways. The one who has lost their Power, seeing another stand in their own Power, will often seek to defeat the one who is standing. This is a natural, instinctual urge. It is also very destructive. The ones who have forgotten often react within their unconscious to antagonize those who stand in their Power. It is for the reason of their innocence feeling what is missing from them and being without the belief that they can achieve it. This creates an emotional response within the individual that becomes anger, primarily without conscious awareness. Within their heart there is a voice calling that they have not listened to. The emotional response cascades into the person's life and is then hidden within their behavior.

Freedom is a necessary aspect of a healthy society. The question, then, is how does one teach responsibility?

To be the example is the test of The Spiritual Warrior. One who speaks yet does not act cannot compare to one who acts and does not speak; yet it is the one whose actions and speech are aligned that upholds The Way. Purpose and preparation play large roles in this work. To be the example is the test and measure of all people.

We must, as a species, learn to be as one peoples with many ways. In this turning of the cycles we are placed upon a precipice within which we may either evolve to be as One or destroy ourselves. To walk as one peoples with many ways is to find the Balance that must be kept. In this, the beginning of the Messianic Age, we can no longer persist in suffering. Our power is too great and our knowledge too vast. To be without wisdom will surely be our end. We will not reach the next cycle without equality, wisdom, and unity. We will not reach the next cycle without reconciliation. We cannot reach for the sky without remembering the Earth. It is the test of all who seek the stars.

The Equation of Leadership

There is an equation in 'Heaven', Who is called Unity, that is the equation of 'fullness'. It is this equation that brings the fullness of Life into this world. To know this equation is also the wisdom which is called Holy. It is this wisdom that all leaders should know, regardless of ideology or doctrine. These are among the principal qualities of this equation:

Freedom is the Spirit's. One cannot dominate the True Nature.

The Spirit cannot find Life without freedom. The tree was not created to be chained to the ground, neither were we created to be other than we are. The fullness of Life is free, for freedom is the Spirit's. We must create the optimal environment for life to flourish. We must teach responsibility and cultivate health. Without freedom the Spirit becomes entrapped and loses its Way. The 'optimal environment' is made with wisdom, being the action of True Knowledge.

A seed planted will bear its fruit

The one who has oppression within themself is one whose equation expresses oppression. The seeds we keep within us express into the world. The seeds we plant become the way we act. A leader must tend to the seeds they plant both within themself and in the world. Through this they may gain the wisdom of leadership.

The one who has not done their inner-work yet seeks to lead will seed into their works the inconsistencies of their inner-world. The inner-work is the origin of wisdom and is a work that all leaders should seek out. The internal environment becomes the external environment. It is the Nature of creation that this is so.

All things are made of equality

Equality is the substance of all creation, for all things come from Oneness. All things are made of equality. To sustain demands recognition of this substantial equality existing in all things. Without equality, and equity in pursuit of equality, the foundation of community is lost. It is for this reason that the leader must humble themself and remember that they are also one of their people. A leader who is not equal has lost the seed of wise leadership.

The Three Fundamental Wisdoms

Through understanding the nature of being human, the nature of good relations, and the nature of individuality one may come to the fundamental wisdom required to sustain a full life. Through developing these three fundamental wisdoms we develop a mentality that can sustain all facets of living. It is wise that these wisdoms should be taught to children and youth.

To understand, at an unconscious level, these three forms of wisdom significantly improves quality of life. When a person deeply understands these forms of wisdom their unconscious integrates them and adapts to include them. It changes behavior at an unconscious level. In order to understand this wisdom we must experience it, for experience is the language of the unconscious.

The Wisdom of Individuality

The one who understands their individuality, who knows themself, understands how they learn; how they choose to live; what brings them peace; how to work with themself, etc.... They develop a connection with their True Nature and their Purpose, clarifying their Way. The one who knows their Self, also, cannot be oppressed in the same way as those who do not know their Self. To teach, then, the wisdom of self-knowledge and self-awareness is a great key to creating fundamental wisdom for good living. It is to develop understanding of the innate individuality that is the essence and fullness of a person's life. This work has often been integrated into cultural and spiritual practices within traditions.

The Wisdom of Good Relations

We are innately in a relationship with all of creation. We are affected by the world around us and we affect the world around us. Our actions move within our environment, rippling into all facets of our life. Our actions ripple, also, into our unconscious. We are directly affected by how we relate to creation. To deeply understand the value of our relationship with all things becomes responsibility. To uphold our relationship with creation maintains our ability to experience the value of life. A person who understands the value of their relationship with the world upholds their place in the world. They create a fulfilling life. Through developing the understanding of the value of upholding they become one who offers respect naturally. The fullness of our place in creation is peace. Our ability to uphold our relationship with the world is directly connected to our capacity for abundance.

The Wisdom of Humanity

To develop the wisdom of humanity is to understand what it means to be human. It is to define how we uphold our humanity and to gather our tools. It is to understand the nature of emotion, mind, spirit, and body. It is to understand how to be in community. It is to understand how we uphold our humanity. In this, the wisdom of humanity is also to understand our downfall. It is to understand our potential for destruction. When we understand what it means to be human it creates a strong foundation for a full life.

Developing the wisdom of individuality, good relations, and humanity creates a strong foundation for a full life. A person who deeply understands these three forms of wisdom will have a significantly better quality of life. To deeply understand these three forms of wisdom is to teach our unconscious to think in alignment with them. The principles that create the improved quality of life individually also apply communally and socially. A social system that teaches the wisdoms of individuality, good relations, and humanity as fundamental knowledge to its children and youth offers them a strong foundation for understanding how to live. When we do not understand how to live we are unable to think in a way that upholds the fullness of our life.

The Lost Place

We built great houses to house ourselves
We shined lights to rival the stars
Blocking our sight to the Heavens and stealing them from the sky
Until only enough remained to remind us of something greater than ourselves

We moved mountains
And burned great forests
We saw the Heavens projected before our eyes
Pictures of the celestial bodies,
We were not satisfied
We created entertainment
Out of metals and crystals
Sent messages around the world in a single instant
We enslaved the minds of the people to this great machine
And consumed the soul of the world

We thought little and knew much
The leader's blind to Truth
For our system only fed the power hungry
We thought little and knew much
And consumed of our self until the body revolted, consuming us in return

We designed chemicals to 'fix' so we did not have to feel
We forgot how to
We invented artificial intelligence to replace that which could be
How long until we forget?
We created our heart's content and were not satisfied
All the things that were only dreams before became reality
And we lost our Way within them

We shined lights to chase away the night
So we lost the Heavens
It was not the darkness to fear
It was our own,
Within it suffering that was left unseen became poison
Yet we remained blind to the Heavens for the lights we had created

Emptied by the world we created
Why did we create it so?
The young taught to not see the forest for the trees
Then growing into that loss
Freedom offered, yet for ignorance long since told as Truth
And forced upon,
Made that it would be
But suffering; our freedom
For wisdom cannot be lost and the wise have found only that

The Earth is dying beneath our feet
While people fall like flies
To the darkness of our poison taking form
In a world poisoned long ago
A power is only as good as the one who wields it
And always cuts both ways
Yet the powerful remain blind to The Way
We continue, in our loss
For the Spirit does not inhabit that lost place

So we burn forests
Blame our peers
Destroy ecosystems
Condemn innocents
And steal the stars from the sky
So we can live in great houses
That never really meant a thing

Mind, Medicine, and Altered States

Perception is illusory. The nature of perception is based in a personal illusion. Our 'illusion' is a face of our Truth. Were two people to look at the same stone from the same location they would perceive two different stones. They would see through different stories. Our beliefs, our memories, our thoughts and patterns, our state of being, shape the way we perceive the world. The greater Truth is that there is a stone while we exist seeing that stone. It is, also, that we exist just as the stone does and that our perception is a part of that innate existence. We, however, can grow distant from alignment with our innate existence. When we grow distant from our innate Truth delusion can fill our 'personal illusion'. The nature of reality is personal and substantial. The nature of perception is a 'personal illusion'..

"The shape of reality begins within"

Creation's movement around us processes through us and from within us reality gains its texture. There is a substantial reality, however it is through the understanding of one's personal illusion and immediate Truth that one may come to understand reality as a whole. We are our own substantial reality. The shape of reality begins within. Our immediate reality is a personal invention.

"To be self-aware is to turn one's gaze towards the Heavens"

All states are altered states. The one who is joyful experiences an altered state filled with joy; the one who is angry and regretful infuses their state with anger and regret. We all walk this Earth with the same chemical messengers in our brain and body. These messengers respond to our conscious directive regarding experience, shaping our experience of reality. The one who is joyful operates in an altered state that is different from the one who is angry and regretful. Their spirit shines in a different light. Joy sends messages of joy; anger sends messages of anger. Both create the person's 'altered state'. The way we respond to joy decides whether it remains a part of our state; the way we respond to anger decides whether it remains a part of our state. A person who speaks experiences the altered state that speech offers them. A person who plays sports or listens to music experiences the altered state of the activity. A person who prays or meditates experiences the altered state of their prayer or meditation. We all exist within an altered state shaped by our experiences, beliefs, preconceptions, actions, nature, heritage, choices, conscious volition, environment, thoughts, words, food, etc… All states are altered states.

All things have medicine. All things shape our 'altered state'. The food we eat; the way we think; what we do; how we speak; the music we listen to, who we speak with, all these things shape our 'altered state'. Our state of being, our 'altered state', is ours to create.

All realities exist in every person to be, however no person can be everything. To find our Self is to know our place in creation.

"To become the creator of our 'altered state' is to come to know the spirit of Self behind it."

Beneath all experience there is a seed of Truth. It is our True Nature manifesting. When we are ours to create, when we are not our experience but are the designer of our experience, we reveal the seed of our existence.

The most pleasing of altered states is peace. Within all people exists the potential for peace. It is to Live fully and that one may uphold their Nature well.

When we come to realize our own Power we also come to recognize that our being is, and always has been, ours to shape.

Our unconscious being weaves together qualities of our existence within its own patterns and principles. The nature of our unconscious self forms our behavior through these weaving qualities. The one who is confident will be more motivated and find greater reward in the things they do. The one who is doubtful will find themself less driven and less rewarded. The neurological system that is associated with confidence is also associated with motivation and reward. The one who can see the beauty of the world, who gives thanks, will feel a deeper sense of connection and a greater sense of joy in their experiences. The one who does not see the beauty of the world, who does not give thanks, will be easily depressed and find that cynicism comes easy. The neurological system that perceives beauty in the world is also the system of joy and connection. The unconscious operates in its own patterns, weaving qualities of behavior and experience together. Our unconscious 'identity' alters the way we behave and experience. If one were to focus on developing drive they would find themself less doubtful. If one were to focus on learning to experience the beauty of life, or to give thanks regularly, they would find themself less depressed.

Conditioning is a natural and normal part of the human experience. It is the unconscious learning from and aligning with its environment. We should not seek to rid ourselves of conditioning, rather we should seek to recondition our unconscious in a way that supports our fullness. Conditioning tethers the mind to a tangible reality that keeps it structured and secured within the vastness of creation. To rid ourselves of conditioning would be to untether the mind.

The way perception operates can be designated into two fundamental processes. These are conditioning and mentality.

Conditioning is the unconscious structure of our being. Incoming information is measured against and associated with our conditioning then processed into active data. Our unconscious, then, offers our interpretation to the conscious mind. The conscious mind uses the processed information to direct its path forward. Conditioning is the unconscious structure of our way of operation. The substance and foundation of our perception is conditioning. Conditioning shifts in accordance with our mentality, among other mental processes. Through our mentality we may reshape our conditioning.

Mentality decides what information we take in. It is a lens through which we see that decides what we see. Mentality can be moved by conscious volition to see in new ways and look to new places. Mentality looks towards its personal understanding of life through the lens of our immediate state. The one who is doubtful looks towards and sees reasons to be doubtful. Their mentality shapes their perception as a lens that changes what they see. The one who is grateful looks towards and sees reasons to give thanks. Their mentality shapes their perception as a lens that changes what they see. Our mentality may, through conscious volition, reshape our conditioning through looking towards that which supports fullness and/or looking toward innate Truth. The one who sees reasons to be doubtful of themself has conditioning that urges their mentality to look towards things that make them doubtful. The one who, in looking towards doubt, turns their sight towards reasons to be empowered will find that their conditioning reshapes to see their Power. Over time looking toward their Power will become natural. It is a pathway of healing. Mentality is an expression of our conditioning and is a 'lens' through which we see the world.

Our perception integrates with our personality. Our personality and behavior is innately intertwined with our perception.

When a person gives thanks their mentality looks towards what they are grateful for. Over time this 'turning of sight' would integrate into conditioning. The conditioning, having been 'reconditioned', would express a mentality that looks towards what it is grateful for. This would express into other facets of the unconscious to improve one's overall experience of life. This shaping our conditioning would, also, express into the personality and behavior of the individual, changing the way they relate to the world. Through turning the sight of the mentality we may recondition our 'self' and integrate a more supportive mental framework for our life.

The one who turns their sight to what they are grateful for also shifts their personality to one that expresses more joy. This person becomes a clearer expression of their Self and a generally happier person.

Our conditioning shapes our environment; our environment shapes our mentality; our mentality shapes our conditioning. The one who is conditioned towards fulfillment walks a path that innately takes them to a more supportive environment. The environment, having changed, then gives the mentality less destructive things to see. The mentality then feeds back into the conditioning, reshaping it again in a constant cycle of generation. To turn one's sight toward good things is a powerful tool in changing one's life.

It is the ability to respond in responsible ways that creates supportive and fulfilling conditioning. This work, which is a work of wisdom, is also a guide through the vastness of The Way.

We all exist within a paradigm. Our paradigm is the conceptual structure of our world. It is a communal conditioning. A paradigm is not inherently good or bad; it is a structure.

Memory weaves us a story of our life. It tells us this thing or that thing and always plays into our ideas of what life means. We weave a story of our memories that then defines our perception. If we feel a deep unease we will weave memories, based on experiences, that tell us a story of dis-ease. If we feel a sense of joy then even the painful memories are but clouds passing on a sunny day. What great power, then, lives in belief and perception that even our memory may be a story told to us. It is as they say 'to those who have, more shall be given; to those who have not, more shall be taken'.

Within all people there is a will that shapes the body and being. This will extends from our life-force. When the mind is free, driven, and knows it can accomplish a thing this will moves. In this movement the unconscious mind orients itself on the task. The unconscious shapes itself in alignment with the choice the person has made when the mind is free, driven, and believes in itself. It is an innate action of the unconscious when the mind is well. All people can accomplish whatever they set their mind to, within reason, for the reason of the body shaping itself in relation to the mind's volition.

Consciousness and intent shape the movement of our being at an energetic level. This reality, of our consciousness shaping our material form, extends even to genetics, reprogramming the body at a fundamental level. We are affected at a fundamental level by the state of our consciousness. Our beliefs, our conscious state, our emotions, our ability to connect, etc… reprogram the body at a fundamental level. Our inner-reality innately shapes the way we live, reprogramming us physically. To step into the fullness of our existence, then, also reprograms the body for a better life. Our thoughts, even, reflect within our body and become the nature of our life, altering our experience.

The body shifts in accordance with the energy surrounding it. Our environment resonates within our body and being, adapting it to our environment.

The majority of thought occurs in the unconscious facets of the mind. Within the unconscious a 'conceptual calculation' is always occurring that, then, informs the conscious mind. The natural state of surface consciousness is one that observes its thoughts. Surface consciousness, however, may become stuck in and attached to its thoughts. This place, in which the surface consciousness becomes its thoughts, is not the natural state of the mind. A person who learns to observe their thoughts honors the natural state of thee mind. This state of mind is a place of greater cognitive ability. The mind, having released its attachment to its thoughts, leaves the unconscious with more space to operate cognitively. The mind gains a greater capacity for complex thought through honoring its natural state. Sacred Silence and meditation are good tools to align the mind with its natural state.

Belief is a powerful tool when integrating new ways of being.

Belief must be grounded in a substantial reality while also expanding into possibility as one seeks to create fulfilling conditioning. The one who believes in fantasy becomes untethered. The one who does not believe in anything becomes dull. The one whose belief is grounded in a substantial reality while also expanding into possibility is wise. Belief is a powerful force. To understand its balance, its medicine, opens many doors.

Our mind is innately connected with our emotions. The way we perceive is intertwined with our emotional wellbeing. A person who seeks to strengthen their mind must also develop emotional wellbeing.

The soul may become burdened. To be burdened is a soulful reality that affects many people directly. Burdens are a source of suffering. They form in our heart from doing evil. The soul, inherently knowing Unity, takes on the burden of its way. To be burdened changes the way we perceive and experience the world even when we are not aware of its impact in our lives. If we are struggling or feel blocked and do not understand why it may be that way we likely carry a burden in our heart. The mind is innately connected to emotion. The expression of emotion comes from our heart. Burdens are kept in the heart and alter the way our emotions express. The work of cleansing burdens and healing the spirit is not an easy work. It takes foundation, compassion, and patience. It remains that our burdens directly affect both our mental and emotional wellbeing.

Burdens can come from places beyond our immediate life. They can pass on generationally, be held in the Universal Memory, or be soulful burdens from other lives. It remains that a burden weighs heavy upon the heart of hearts, changing the way we experience and act within our life.

The one who acts in cruelty, resentment, division, etc.. takes on a burden that blinds them to Truth. Their state becomes infused with their burden, causing suffering within their heart of hearts for their ways. Should they remain numb to their burdens their potential for peace, and for True Balance, is lost. When they choose to heal they will also feel the impact of what they have inflicted on others, even should they be numb to feeling in this moment. That which does not feel its Truth cannot find its peace. There is always consequence, for All is One.

To release a burden demands True reconciliation. This True reconciliation is to earn the forgiveness of our soul and transform into the freedom that comes after genuine acknowledgement. The burden will not respond to the healing journey.

Suffering impacts our ability to experience the value of life. It becomes easy to forget that there is a life beyond suffering. Suffering affects, also, our unconscious urges and impulses. This occurs regardless of our acknowledgement.

To seek peace and the will to embrace wholly the upholding of Balance is a guiding light in the work of releasing burdens. To seek peace directs a person to the place of fullness. To be willing to embrace wholly the upholding of Balance is to open the door for the transformation of self into Self.

Emotion plays a large role in the mind, shaping our state of being. Emotion is the savor of life, yet often it becomes a poisoned Truth. In those who have come to carry great burdens emotion is a difficult experience. The one who learns to keep their emotions, creating peace within themself, is also one who has honed their mind. This one, who upkeeps their emotions, has learned to keep the savor of life and their world becomes vibrant

Our mind is intertwined with the rest of our being. When we are not present with the realities of our spirit, our emotions, and our body our mind cannot be well.

We are beings of creation. It is through self-creation that we create the world.

“Thoughts lead to patterns, patterns lead to behaviors, behaviors lead to ways of living. The way we think is the way we live.”

- Anishinaabe Teaching

We are designed naturally to seek peace and turn away from pain. When a person is completely aware of the effects of an action, and is not interpreting through suffering, they turn towards the most pleasing action. The most pleasing action is always the one that brings us to peace and health. A person who eats junk food, when healthy and aware, will repeatedly learn that junk food makes them sick. They will naturally turn towards good food, should they be healthy and aware. We seek transient pleasure in unconscious ignorance of the pain it causes us and as an expression of our suffering. We are designed naturally to seek peace and turn away from pain.

To teach the unconscious to perceive the fullness of what aids us and what hurts us is a great key. Believing that transient pleasure is something pleasing, or liberating, allows our conditioning to continue in the pursuit of what destroys us. We are designed to seek peace, not transient pleasure. In True Knowledge the unconscious seeks peace in the understanding that peace is consistently pleasing to the senses while transient pleasure eventually leads to pain. When we Truly believe that peace is the source of what pleases us we align with our True Nature and we no longer permit self-destruction. At this point we must also walk our healing journey and reconcile.

There are many ways of perceiving the world. To open our perception to another's viewpoint is not only a gate to Knowledge, it is also an important part of finding peace. All viewpoints, all places in the circle, have their Life. We all take our own place in the circle and each is valuable. Each viewpoint has its own medicine. The Spirit speaks in many ways and has many voices. The one who cannot hear the voice of wisdom from the mouth of a beggar has yet to Know, for they are proud within their heart. There are many ways of perceiving the world. The one who is open to another's viewpoint, remembering that Balance is The Way, upholds the substance of creation. To see in this way clarifies our 'altered state' and expresses a more peace-filled mentality.

When we bring ill will into the world we reflect illness into our 'self'. We become ill for the sake of spreading illness.

All things change our state of being. All things are medicine. The things we take in alter the way we perceive the world, even to the extent of sight and sound. A 'psychoactive' medicine is very powerful in this shifting of one's state. It remains that all things alter our state of consciousness and are medicine for this reason. To create a pleasing altered state is also to be present with what one is taking in. To listen to poisonous music will infuse one's state with poison; to watch toxic things will infuse one's state with toxicity; to act in ways that are ill will infuse one's state with illness.

Everything has its medicine. It is when we do not respect the medicine of a thing that it becomes toxic to us. The sun warms us and gives us minerals, yet when we stay too long in its light we grow sick. It is, also, that even poisons can be used in beneficial ways. Everything has its medicine.

People also exist in this way, with a medicine that is their own. The fullness of their medicine is the upholding of their True Nature. It is when we abuse the medicine of a thing that it becomes toxic to us. Within this toxic relationship we also become toxic. Respect is a powerful healing force.

To challenge one's thoughts with wisdom and understanding aids the unconscious being in developing a peaceful equilibrium from which to operate in life. This work, of challenging thoughts, is best done as we seek to align with our True Nature, reconcile, and walk our healing journey. When one thinks destructive thoughts, such as self-defeating thoughts, to leave them unchallenged leads to one's destruction. To challenge thoughts with wisdom and support for one's inner-nature opens the opportunity for healing to occur. Through this one may come to a greater sense of peace in life. The one who defeats themself without challenge will always be defeated; the one who always challenges their own defeat is one who will never be defeated.

To do the inner-work is also to work with our own nature. The one who turns their gaze inward will see themself reflected.

Our inner-nature is filled with reflections of who we are. As our unconscious grows is uses images of who we were at different stages of our life to mark growing cycles. Our unconscious stores information through applying images of who we were at different stages of our life. It is as rings on a tree within our unconscious. One who is spiritually aware may look within and have these 'little selves' speak to them. It is the unconscious being seeking the conscious volition. When we are working to challenge thoughts we are also challenging the 'little self' that holds the origin of that thought process within us. We are challenging who we were at the age we first gained that thought process. We work with the logic of a younger version of our own nature. To change our thought patterns may require that we heal the younger version of ourself so that our unconscious is willing to release the attachment that holds the process in place.

When we are triggered we may become a younger version of ourself. We may become the little self who holds the wound. It is important, if this occurs, that we remember what we are grateful for and what we love about ourself.

Mind is the vehicle consciousness uses to move within creation.

There is space within us. We are a circle filled with the state of our being. Our state of being in this moment fills the space of our circle. In order to create change we must both give away that which does not serve us and fill that space with what supports and sustains us. This space is a set amount. You cannot fill a space that is already full. When we give away, the space that is created may fill itself with its memory. As we seek to progress in our life we must both move out and take in. This completes the circle.

As we seek to create peace in our lives we must look for actions to take. To work within is only one aspect of healing. To take an action from our inner-work anchors transformation into the physical world.

Flow exists in all things always. What we call the creative Flow-State is a state within which our unconscious aligns with a greater movement. This state is also the state of the enlightened. The enlightened 'flow' within their spirit, becoming emptied into fullness. The creative empties themself into their flow, expressing their spirit. In the place of flow the unconscious has become aligned with the spirit of its conception. Peace exists in that place. This peace is the True Nature expressing. Flow is a dance with the Spirit of Creation, moving into alignment with our Self. Just as the musician flows in their rhythm so too do we play the song of our soul.

The will and intent, when applied with good method, consistency, and persistence, may shape and reshape the entirety of the mind's faculties. The brain is malleable, shaping in response to our way of being. It is this principle that, when applied with wisdom, creates a new way of operation.

There are facets of the mind and brain that modern humanity does not use. These facets atrophy when they are not used, however they remain present within. The work of opening these capacities is strongly related to the works of spiritual medicine and magic. It is a very sacred work to learn to open one's mind.

It is possible to awaken the ability to use more of one's Natural capacity. This work requires that a person pursues and aligns with Truth. To awaken more of the Natural capacity of the mind begins with becoming one's Self. It is a mental, emotional, physical, and spiritual work.

There is a temple hidden within the unconscious. The unconscious is a sacred instrument of creation. When we learn to work with our unconscious being we are also entering its temple.

Sacred Silence is a great key in the temple of the mind.

A mind without detachment cannot see even that which is direct were it not within its 'thought' to exist. This one, who cannot observe purely and without preconception, is blind to the gate of True Knowledge.

Not one may achieve the fullness of their mental capacity without taking into account the entirety of their life. The state of being and feeling well is not solely mental. It is emotional, spiritual, physical, soulful, relative, etc… It is all the things we do that go into our 'altered state'. To reach one's fullest capacity is to attain self-mastery.

Mental health is a full life.

Consciousness and The Unconscious

Our way of action and behavior is a product of our unconscious state. A person can have the best of intents, however if their unconscious is not aligned with their intent they will not be able to uphold. We must align our unconscious with the intent of our fullness. Life-force is constantly expressing from our soul and into our unconscious. The urge of life is as water running through the ingrained pathways of our unconscious. Through this our way of action and behavior is created. It is within this relationship that we can find the reason behind the thoughts we hear when we step into Sacred Silence. Life-force moves within the Truth of what is within our unconscious and creates our thoughts. In this, it also creates our way of action and behavior. We must shape our unconscious into the image of our fullness, our Self. We are a product of our unconscious state.

Within Consciousness we may perceive two direct expressions. These are: Surface Consciousness and The Unconscious.

Within the Surface Consciousness we may perceive two expressions. They are: The Immediate Self and The Voice of The Observer

Within The Unconscious we may perceive six expressions: These are: The Energy Body, The Emotion Body, The Energetic Nature, The Unconscious Processes, The Life-Force, and The Brain and Body.

The Immediate Self

The immediate self is the entirety of our immediate state of being amalgamating within our surface consciousness as our personality. Our immediate self, through this amalgamation, creates an immediate sense of identity and a framework that allows the unconscious state to operate through the surface consciousness. Our immediate self is a house our soul has built around itself to know the world. Our immediate self is ours to create.

The Voice of The Observer

Within the Surface Consciousness there is a voice that is distinct from the thoughts that occur due to the life-force moving within the unconscious processes. A person in Sacred Silence, and who has clarity, will be able to discern a voice coming from their Surface Consciousness. This voice is The Voice of The Observer. It is the voice of our spirit and our Self. When we have aligned our unconscious with the direction of our 'observer' we have aligned with our True Nature. When we have aligned with the voice of our observer we gain clarity.

The Energy Body - Spirit

We have an energy body that is the energetic realities of our being manifesting. Beneath the surface-center of creation, the material world, all things are energetic manifestations. Just as we are a complex material system, so too are we a complex energetic system. Our energy body is where we find chakras and other energetic realities. What exists within our energy body is stored within the brain and body. A person who works with their energy body changes what is stored in their brain and body. The energy body is a substantial energetic reality, existing in all people.

The Emotion Body - Emotion

As our soul relates to the world it creates an emotion body that is as a fundamental algorithm for how we respond to our experiences. It is an energetic 'entity' that represents our emotional connection with the world around us. The emotion body may become wounded. A person who is healthy emotionally has an emotion body that clearly reflects the nature of their soul's relationship with the world.

The Energetic Nature - Body

Our energetic nature is how our unconscious stores the energies and emotions we carry. A person who carries much suffering would have much suffering in their energetic nature. The energetic nature has a set amount of space. A person with much suffering would not be able to experience the full joy of life because the space of their energetic nature would be filled by that suffering. A person who has much anger stores their anger in their energetic nature. A person who has much sadness would store their sadness in their energetic nature. The goal when working with the energetic nature is clarity. The energies stored in our energetic nature are reflected in our brain and body as chemical messengers. A person who works to release suffering releases it from their energetic nature and their brain and body.

The Unconscious Processes - Mind

Thought patterns are ingrained pathways within the unconscious, defined by what the unconscious has integrated. These intent-defined pathways of thought are the unconscious processes. A person who believes they are unworthy has unconscious processes that create thoughts in relation to the belief. A person who believes they are worthy becomes clear. The unconscious processes are the integrated patterns and processes that define how thought occurs within us. Life-force moves within the unconscious processes and creates a wind that results in our thoughts.

The Life-Force

Within us, a constant energetic charge moves within and through the ingrained patterns of our unconscious. This constant energetic charge is our life-force. Our life-force fills our immediate state, bringing life into our body and being.

The Brain and Body

That which exists within our unconscious reflects the information stored in our brain and body. Our unconscious is as its own energetic dimension. Our brain and body store our unconscious state.

The Process of Focus, Awareness, and Attention

Focus, Awareness, and Attention are a single process within the mind. Within the unconscious focus, awareness and attention are all parts of a single mental process. When capacity increases within this process it increases for all aspects of the process. The increasing of strength within the mental process indicates a strong capacity for awareness and a strong capacity for focus. The spirit is strong within the mental process. This strength is capable of both pulling a mind away from what it is not interested in and drawing the mind far into what it is interested in. The strength of the dynamic creates a more difficult 'balance point' to hold and so requires greater poise to uphold. This is the nature of all spiritual gifts.

Our inner-eye perceives a landscape through our eyes.

Awareness is the ability to be present with the entire landscape. It is to see the bird flying through the air; the otter in the creek; the squirrel jumping from tree to tree.

Focus is our ability to remain mentally poised on a single aspect of the landscape. Focus is the ability to hold one's sight on a single object within the landscape.

Attention is where we are turning our inner-eye. Attention is where we attend to, whether it be a focal point or awareness. It is the presence of our inner-eye.

Focus and awareness exist in a spectrum. They are not separate forces. They are two faces of the same force. As one attends to focus their awareness remains present; as one attends to awareness their focus remains present. The one who focuses on the otter in the creek noticed the otter through awareness. Without that awareness they could not have gained that focal point. To be aware opens the inner-eye to new realities while focus directs our energy towards a single reality. Focus and awareness work in tandem. One without the other creates imbalance. As the capacity of one increases so too does the capacity of the other.

Those who 'struggle to focus', who are in this world said to have ADHD, carry the gift of The Hunter. The hunter would have to be attentive to their surroundings so, out of necessity, developed strength in their capacity for awareness. The strength they developed in awareness, for the reason of the nature of the mental process, also developed a strong capacity for focus. The strength within the process makes it so that the hunter either has to be genuinely interested in what they're doing or must learn to hone their mind on their objective. Without this action of 'honing the mind' it can appear as though a person is struggling to focus when, truly, they are just not interested in what they're doing. The gift of The Hunter becomes a blessing when upheld in its nature.

When a person with the gift of The Hunter finds a focal point they tend to 'tunnel vision'. Without a focal point that develops their ability to access this state of heightened focus it can become difficult for one gifted in the way of The Hunter to access their capacity for focus. Their strength in the process of focus, awareness, and attention pulls them away from things that do not interest them. When they find their focal point and 'tunnel vision' they may use the activity to teach themself to hone their focus on other activities if they choose. This 'bridging' is best achieved when the value of the action to their own wellbeing is deeply understood. The Hunter may learn to access their capacity for focus by finding a viable focal point then bridging the focus into other activities.

Balance is The Way. As capacity increases so too does the degree of poise required to maintain Balance. The nature of a spiritual gift is that a 'process' holds a greater 'innate' capacity. A person with ADHD is gifted, yet it also carries an equal 'burden'. When we do not learn to maintain the burden of our spiritual gifts they appear as though they are illness, however the illness is not in the process. It is in our inability to maintain good Balance in relation to the spiritual gift. The illness is not in the process. It is in the inability to maintain the process appropriately. A person with ADHD, with the gift of The Hunter, gains a great blessing when they learn to uphold their spiritual gift well.

Psychoactive Medicines

Medicines used to enter altered states, 'psychoactive' medicines, facilitate a connection with new ways of living in the ones who use them. This is a very powerful action. It is for the reason of this power that psychoactive medicines may destroy wholly those who do not approach them with proper respect. When the facilitation with a new way of living becomes the only way to see that new life a person loses themself within the medicine they are using. The external substance becomes the only means to achieve that state of being. This becomes addiction.

The Power of psychoactive medicines is a power akin to ceremonial tools. It is a power altered states innately hold. This is why a person that works with psychoactive medicines must be very conscious of the medicine they are using. They must understand the fullness of their action. Much as a ceremonial tool can injure a person who does not uphold it properly, so too do psychoactive medicines require good understanding to prevent injury.

Psychoactive medicines can be well understood as Gateways, Pathways, and Teachers. When we approach them in this way it helps us find a place beyond the need of them. To approach them in this way shows respect to their Power and helps us step into new life.

Gateway

The gateway of a psychoactive medicine is the opening of the mind to a new way of living. As a person enters into a new state of consciousness they release their hold on their idea of life. The mind awakens to new realities that it did not understand before. Through this 'awakening' the mind releases its attachment to its previous understanding.

Pathway

To uphold a psychoactive medicine is a pathway we walk into a new way of living. When we walk this pathway it becomes a way we overcome the medicine's hold over us. The new way of living we search for must be a way that is not dependent on the medicine. A person with self-doubt may drink alcohol. Were they to use alcohol as a way to overcome self-doubt the alcohol would lose power over them. The pathway that exists within a medicine is an internal journey within which we learn to step into the place where we no longer need to facilitate the connection with the state that exists within us. In this way the pathway that exists in a medicine can be a healing journey within which we step into the version of ourself that does not need it to feel well. When we do not walk this pathway the medicine becomes the only way to access the state of being. We, then, become dependent on the medicine to facilitate a connection with a way of living that feels more full.

"Psychoactive medicines don't add anything new into the brain. They only alter the balance of what is already there."

We all have within us all realities already existing. A psychoactive medicine, such as alcohol or marijuana, only alters the balance of the messengers already present within us. We already have within us the life we seek to live. It is ours to create.

Teacher

Every psychoactive medicine carries teachings within its upholding. These teachings create a new way of living. To listen to the teachings of a medicine is to integrate what they offer us. To use alcohol to facilitate socialization is the medicine teaching us to let go of inhibition. A person who learns to let go of their inhibitions without the need of alcohol, and with self-control, has learned the teachings of the medicine. To use a 'big teacher', a psychedelic, teaches us of creation's mysteries. To use a 'painkiller' offers room for healing. To use an 'empathogen' is also to learn about healing one's heart. Each medicine carries within it qualities that the unconscious uses to compensate for its 'imbalances'. The teaching of the medicine is also that we may learn to overcome our 'imbalances'.

A 'psychedelic' medicine is a big teacher. They teach us and help us open our minds. They are a Powerful prayer when used with wisdom. The one who honors a big teacher for the teachings they offer opens their mind to the Spirit of Creation.

It is my belief that there is divine purpose in plant medicines. I believe that one of the reasons we have medicines that ease pain is because Creator saw us in pain and wanted to ease our suffering.

It is the nature of suffering to compensate and cope. Addiction is a symptom of suffering.

The one who does not learn, who does not progress beyond their immediate way, will find little help in altered states. The one who grows and evolves through altered states, moving into a life that does not abuse the medicines, may find a powerful ally and medicine within them.

Altered states can open doors to worlds in Spirit. When we step into another world, which often occurs while still in our own body, it is a sacred journey. To misunderstand this sacredness leads to madness. One may step into a spirit world without understanding they are doing so. This opening remains a sacred journey in the worlds beyond our own. The one who steps upon this journey foolishly will be made to uphold Balance whether they want to or not. Should they not uphold, the repercussion is also of the other worlds. There is a great Power and sacredness in altered states that is akin to ceremonial tools. To abuse a ceremonial tool leads to great sickness.

When we do not honor the Purpose and Balance of a medicine we are taken far into the opposite direction of its principles. To not uphold a painkiller takes one far into pain; to not uphold a 'big teacher' (a psychedelic) sends one far into the spirit world; to not uphold an empathogen takes one far into emotional imbalance.

The Heart's Balance

There was once a great man who was beloved by all. The earth wept at his passage and his people could not be consoled. In his life he gave and in his life he wore a crown of wisdom and integrity.

He awakes in darkness. A path is laid out before him leading through a mountain pass. A darkness weighs on all sides of the pass as though nothing else exists. He feels his ancestors around him, comforting him. He knows in that moment that there is no turning back. He is not afraid for himself. His heart is concerned only for those he left behind. 'May they find peace' he thinks. He begins to walk.

As he walks through the mountain pass he sees strangers by the wayside. They look starved and weary. When he sees them his spirit grows in strength and he carries on.

Shadows laugh in the mountains, whispering his name. Their laughter is shrill. It strikes fear into his innermost Truth. His spirit grows in strength and he carries on.

He keeps walking, accompanied by his ancestors and all those who walked this pass before him who saw his life and loved him.

As he walks he sees an old friend by the wayside. His friend is digging into the earth at the foot of a mountain calling out 'I just need some!'. The sound is a distant echo, resonating in his mind as he focuses on it. He stops for his friend.

They look back and see him in return. Their eyes are glazed; their hands bloodied from digging; their body starved and ragged. The clothes that once adorned them are ripped and stained.

"Jeremiah!" he whispers softly. The sound passes through the mountains and returns to him. Shadows laugh in the distance. His old friend acknowledges him. The blank eyes gain clarity for a moment, remembering.

Jeremiah's eyes return to a blank gaze and fill with rage. "There is no love here; no life!" Jeremiah spits out with contempt.

The man knows his friend as a good man who did great things in their community. He hears a voice speak from the empty space around him, *'walk on, beloved, walk on.'* It sounds as though the voice of his grandmother, entreating him to continue.

"Give me your water" Jeremiah says coldly, There is no room for compromise in his voice. The man watches his old friend,

'Continue on' calls the grandmother again.

"Give me your water!" Jeremiah's features contort. His face becomes dark and monstrous. He reaches out from the wayside. As Jeremiah's hand comes close to the man, paralyzed and watching, a light ripples between them. Jeremiah pulls his hand back, clutching it like he had been struck.

"Give me your water!" He yells, yet it sounds more distant than a whisper.

"Continue on' speaks the grandmother one last time. Her voice is soft and gentle.

The man turns to continue his path through the mountains, turning his back on his old friend.

"I will not forget this! You will never live again! You are dead like me!" Jeremiah yells after him.

All the man hears is the shrill laughter of the shadows that hide in the mountains as he walks away.

As he grows farther from his old friend he picks himself up, shaking off the weight he'd taken on. His spirit grows in strength and he carries on.

He passes others on his way. They are all lost. He wonders how they could be lost with a path laid down before them. He is saddened by this, for he sees their pain and knows he cannot help them.

"Find peace," speaks the grandmother. "*They are where they are meant to be, where they have created for themself"*

"Why am I different?" the man thinks.

There is a brief moment before a gentle and powerful response. *"Who says you are..."* The voice is not the grandmother's. It is tough and rigid. There is warmth beneath the hardness of the voice.

Eventually, after what feels like eternity, he comes to a gate. It is where the mountain pass ends. The gate is massive and imposing. On all sides of the gate there is No-Thing. A pedestal rests in front of the gate. Upon the pedestal an old scale, covered in webs and with dull metal, sits. The image provokes a fear within the man's innermost Truth. An inner-voice calls from within his heart for more time. His spirit grows in strength. He turns toward the pedestal and carries on.

A giant shadow steps out of the No-Thing beside the gate. The man sees, briefly, the eyes of the being. They are calm and contemplative, golden and filled with an eternal wisdom. It is not love; it is not kindness; yet it is surely something to be revered.

The man tries to look closer at the being, yet each time he focuses the image escapes him. He catches a glimpse of a man with a canine's head, adorned with golden vestments.

"Are you ready?" the great being asks the man, mouth unmoving. His voice is thunder.

"I am" speaks the man, his spirit growing in strength. Within him a small voice calls out, 'I need more time!'

The man sees himself appear on the other side of the scale. He stands there, looking back towards himself. The man's reflection draws a dagger from the pedestal. Its blade is black obsidian. Calmly, he cuts open his chest and draws out a star. He places his star heart on the scale then crumbles and turns to dust.

Upon the scale his star heart shines. Swimming in its light the man can see his life. A sadness rises within him. He cannot see the light for the regret it awakens within him.

The god appears in front of the gate. The god raises his hand high above and plucks a feather from the sky, bringing it down upon the other side of the scale.

Slowly the scale tips over toward the man's star heart.

His innermost Truth cries out: 'I need more time!'

As the scale falls the vision fades. The pedestal and the scale become sand, carried away in the wind.

A sacred Silence fills the space. The man stands before the god.

They speak, mouth unmoving. **"You are not ready."**

The great man, his heart dropping and his fear rising, feels a deep knowledge well up within him. He knows he is not ready.

His burdens pass as visions before his eyes. He remembers the ones he had watched burn so his own may live. His regrets well up within him. All the giving; all the good and still he was not free. He always worked to redeem yet never forgave.

He falls to his knees and weeps. *"I was not ready"* he speaks calmly, a soft grief filling his words. *"I am sorry"*

The great one watches him. **"You will return"** The words echo out across the mountains, into the void, out to the end of creation, then return again.

The great being returns to the shadow of the gate.

The man remains on his knees, weeping.

The mountains go silent. The shadows watch him from a distance.

Soon he is only dust in the wind. His essence carried to another life where he might find The Way.

"One of the greatest steps onto the Wayside is that we think ourselves great and not the Spirit within us"

"Magic, in its purest form, is the movement of the Power of creation"

"In old ways of thought the medicine person had to gain the approval of the spirits"

Magic, Energy, and The Spirit World

Magic, Energy, and The Spirit World introduces readers to teachings relating to the works of Spirit. The works of Spirit are the works of magic, medicine, and mystery. To work with Spirit is to become 'one who Knows'. Through aligning with and understanding the mysteries of creation a person becomes able to work with Spirit. Through Knowledge a person becomes a magic wielder and/or medicine person. In Magic, Energy, and The Spirit World many fundamental teachings are shared that introduce readers to the realities surrounding the work of the medicine person and/or magic wielder. .

Underneath the surface-center of creation, the material world, worlds of Spirit and energy exist. The energetic domains of creation are the worlds of Spirit. These worlds are the unconscious of creation. One who Truly works with Spirit experiences and sustain the experience of the energetic realities of creation. They see that which is unseen. Through this they become able to work with energy, divine The Way, heal, speak with spirits, etc....

Spirit is the energetic manifestation of creation. Spirit is the name we have given to our experience of energetic reality.

Those who seek to be gifted by Spirit for things such as sight and Power should seek first to pray, asking for that Way and guidance through it. Any and all people may call in those who would gift them these Powers, however that does not mean that the gift will be given. One should persist in good will, then, for good will and persistence are highly regarded.

The works of Spirit are sacred works. They are the works of magic, medicine, and mystery. They are the works of the healer; of the medicine person; of the 'priest or priestess', etc...

It is wise to understand that this work becomes much more difficult without a temple/way that knows it, an environment that acknowledges it, and a community that supports it.

The works of Spirit should not be sought after in the idea of personal gain and power. The one who seeks in the idea of personal gain and power will find that their work leads them to their own destruction. It is, even, that one must approach the works of Spirit without expectation. The one who seeks personal gain will find that any success only leads to greater downfall. This Truth, however, does not mean that one should not seek to sustain their life with their spiritual work. It means that worldly ideas of wealth are not thoughts that the Spirit abides. To practice the works of Spirit is a calling. It is not a power. The works of Spirit are works of service.

All of Spirit's gifts are borrowed. The gifts of magic, medicine, and mystery are given from Spirit to create and sustain Balance.

The works of Spirit are not about being perfect. They are, rather, a calling within which a person seeks the fullness of their life through their study. The one who is not liberated by Spirit has yet to understand Their work. The fullness of the work is a place of rest.

The works of Spirit can cause injury when not approached with proper respect. Spiritual injuries are often called 'mental illness', however that does not mean every mental illness is a spiritual injury. If one seeks the gifts of Spirit it is wise to first contemplate this choice within the Sacred Silence, that it may be considered with wisdom and depth.

One who Truly studies the Spirit cannot help but to create Power.

The traditional medicine person must gain the approval of the spirits and Spirit to work with magic and spiritual medicine.

Spirit often tests the resolve of those who seek Them. The practitioner can be pushed to their limits by Spirit. It is a way that a practitioner gains Their approval.

The works of Spirit can be painful. The 'awakenings' that must occur can be painful for the body and being. They can push the mind to its limits. This pain is called Medicine Pain. It is for this reason that the willingness to face pain and remain stable is one of the ways that the spirits test those who seek these works.

The spirits prize the good hearted people. The good hearted one is the one who honors The Way and respects all of Life. One who comes into the works of Spirit without the will to be good of heart, or create goodwill within themself, is likely to injure themself.

We all have a good heart within us. It lives underneath our suffering. The one who seeks to reveal their good heart should seek their healing journey and reconcile.

One may participate in spiritual realities without seeking to become a practitioner. There is a difference between immersing oneself in Spirit and learning to live in alignment with ones spiritual, energetic, Nature. We are all spirits that walk in matter. Regardless of being spiritual we are still energetic systems of expression and interconnection. To work with and acknowledge spiritual realities without becoming a medicine person is to allow them to remain peripheral. The medicine person seeks direct connection with Spirit so immerses themself in the unseen.

Prayer is not meant for personal gain. Prayer is meant as a way to connect with higher powers and as a way that we might ask to do and be supported in our good work, our Way. We are not meant to pray for personal gain. We are meant to pray that we may grow as a person, for the support we need along our Way, or to support others in achieving their fullness..

The works of Spirit, of magic, medicine, and mystery, can be separated into two expressions. These expressions are: The Ways of Wisdom and The Ways of Power.

The Ways of Wisdom are filled with the fundamental Knowledge, practices, and teachings that help a person sustain a full life. The Ways of Wisdom are the wisdom teachings that help a person live well in relation to the mysteries. Cleansing rituals, traditional wisdom teachings, breathing techniques, routine, meditation/prayer/gnosis, etc… are Ways of Wisdom.

The Ways of Power are the works of Spirit that carry great Power. It is within the Ways of Power that great secrets take place within the life of the practitioner, shaping them into the Power that exists within their spirit. These ways are often hidden from the unwise for the sake of their potential to create destruction in both the life of the unwise practitioner and the world that practitioner attempts to practice within.

The True work begins, always, in the Ways of Wisdom and eventually leads into the Ways of Power. One who Truly studies wisdom will arrive at The Ways of Power.

To seek The Ways of Power before The Ways of Wisdom becomes the destruction of one's spirit.

In the works of Spirit, being the works of magic, medicine, and mystery, there is The Way and the Wayside.

The Way has no name, so we call it The Way. The Way has many names throughout many cultures and traditions. The Way is alignment with Natural Law, with Creator and Spirit. The Way is the heart of the works of Spirit. One who does not study The Way will not find the Spirit.

The Wayside is a place where those who do not walk The Way, or those who have lost their Way, rest. It is the place where a person no longer pursues the fullness of Life.

"One of the great steps onto the Wayside is that we think ourselves great and not the Spirit within us."

The old ways of medicine and magic are still watched over by those who knew them well. When we step into a practice of a way of knowing we are seen by these old ones. They often welcome the calling of those who see them well.

"Unity is the heart of all magic"

All things began as One. The innate Power of creation is Oneness. The heart of all mysteries is Oneness. The place of highest attainment is also the point of Supreme Balance. Energy and Power come from the point of Supreme Balance.

There is a wisdom within all things that is the upholding of its utmost potential within the principles of Oneness. Through understanding the wisdom of a thing a person may gain much insight. Through gaining insight one may reveal their own wisdom.

We all have a wisdom that we may connect to as we continue in our life. Our wisdom is the 'knowing', the way of thought, of our True Nature. We may turn to our wisdom to help guide us through difficult times. This is well achieved through asking: 'what does my wisdom say about this thing?' while contemplating the answer in a calm state of mind. To ask this question and take a moment to contemplate the answer is very helpful.

When magic and spiritual medicine are not applied in pursuit of Balance, both individually and universally, there is a threefold consequence that occurs within Spirit. The three folds of this consequence are: Reflection, Integration, and Counter-Balance.

Reflection: The qualities of the energetic movement are reflected back to the practitioner.

Integration: The qualities of the energetic movement are integrated into the unconscious of the practitioner.

Counter-Balance: The potential consequence of an energetic movement is increased by how conflicted the movement is against Natural Law. The Spirit 'counter-balances' an energetic movement depending upon how much the movement moves against Their Nature.

To practice any form of magic demands that a practitioner keep foundation and learn fundamental spiritual practices. The foundation that is required of a practitioner is fulfilled in the ways of operation, both internal and external, that sustain the fullness of their life in relation to their practice. To work magic without routine, wisdom, discipline, discernment, consistency, and fundamental practices, such as cleansing rituals, is much like building a tower on sand. Personal upkeep operates as a form of foundation, creating the means to sustain magical works.

Healing work is fundamental to sustain a full magical practice. The practitioner who does not walk their healing journey and reconcile is standing on a broken leg expecting not to fall.

There is a world in Spirit. There are boundaries, customs, and rules in that place. It is wise to understand that even though one may not perceive where they are in Spirit there are still boundaries and customs in that world. The spirit world is not our world. It is why we often need a guide to walk within it. There are many repercussions that may occur when a person's spirit is not welcome in a world they are walking in. If one thinks they are experiencing repercussions for walking where they are not welcome it is wise to ask for guidance from a spirit guide or helper. They see that side and can help us know where we are and if we are welcome there. There can be great repercussions given to people, even in ignorance, for stepping into worlds they are not welcome in.

That a person has entered a world in Spirit they are not welcomed in is one of the potential destructions of altered states. The altered state is a prayer vehicle that has great capacity to open doors for spiritual travel. If a person is abusing altered states it is likely their spirit will begin traveling.

Divination is a form of communion in a similar way to prayer being a form of communion. The one who practices astrology, even, is communing with the celestial bodies to discern the nature of the path ahead. The one who gazes into fire is seeking to commune through the fire to gain clarity regarding the path ahead. The one who prays is communing with greater beings, whether to gain clarity or ask for help. Divination practices are a form of communion with the Spirit of Creation, offering a way for Them to speak to and guide us.

*Communion here refers to communication and the sharing/coming together of energetic spaces

The art and practice of divination is an opening of a channel to the Spirit of Creation and to the spirits that take interest in our lives. It is wise to understand that one is seeking to communicate with the Spirit and Their many faces through their method of divination. It is not so much about what is exactly within the future so much as that which is being spoken by Spirit. To approach divination as a method of communication with Spirit helps to clarify the messages being received.

When Spirit speaks through divination Their signs pertain to the individual who is requesting guidance. A practitioner who is divining for another should seek to offer, as clearly as possible, the signs offered to them. An interpretation should only be given if requested, however can be offered.

To practice divination it is wise that a practitioner learns to enter a form of Sacred Silence. The Sacred Silence facilitates a connection to 'altered states' that allow communion to occur. The Spirit tends to need this form of connection in order to commune with clarity. These 'altered states' may appear naturally for a practitioner whose practice includes wisdom teachings, has past-life experience with medicine and magic, or has medicine people in their lineage.

When a person seeks to participate in magical or spiritual works it is wise to have a method of communion between the Spirit and the practitioner. This method of communion can be prayer, divination, meditation, trance, gnosis, etc… The goal is to have a practice that allows connection and communion with Spirit.

The Way is here and now. It is the building of here and now. It is within the moment that Eternity exists.

All words, signs, images, visions from Spirit are 'translated' through our state of being and way of knowing. The expression of Spirit translates through our 'personal illusion'. This 'translation' that occurs can leave much to interpretation.

It is, also, that Spirit speaks to us through our stories and to guide us along our own journey.

A miracle is a form of magic.

The speech of the soul is the universal language. Its words are carried on the energetic force of unconditional love. All things speak soul speech. Soul speech is senses and images. It is Silent and interconnected. When we learn to speak and listen with the heart and soul we become able to speak and listen in soul speech. It is at this point that we may speak to the plants, animals, and elements. It is at this point that we may commune with all things.

When a practitioner is aligned with their soulful nature to the extent that their Silence speaks through them they may speak in tongues. To speak these tongues is prayer. Tongues occur when the heart and soul have chosen to speak and skip translation. Tongues are not meant for all people to hear, rather it is a way that we commune with Creator and, depending on our way of knowing, with the spirits and deities. To speak tongues is to pray. It is to become prayer.

We are not allowed to apply spiritual Power to help others without receiving permission. There are many things that come before applying one's Power to helping others.

In traditional ways of thought, which should be upheld to one's best ability, a practitioner should reach mastery before teaching. It is for the reason of the Power of teachings to create injury that this is so.

The medicine of forces beyond us is not ours to take. We must ask for medicine through creating a relationship. When we are seeking silver from Grandmother Moon, for instance, we must build a relationship with her spirit, create a vessel, and ask for the medicine within an appropriate time and space. A good way to create this relationship is to moon gaze. When we are working with crystals we must ask for their help and do our best to be present with the answer. A good way to accomplish this is to sit with the crystal in the Sacred Silence. The medicine of forces beyond us is not ours to take; it is theirs to give.

To align one's unconscious with Natural Law is the foundation of the works of Spirit.

There are spiritual predators that stalk the spirit world. Possession is a real occurrence. The one who has become the prey of spiritual predators is fed upon for their poisons and burdens. These predators would do their best to keep these poisons and burdens within the individual so that they may keep their prey. To overcome this sickness, which is possession, one must find within the will and/or the help they need to overcome both their own 'illness' and the predators that prey upon them. To overcome possession is to overcome both the illness and the spirits that feed upon it.

Though the works of Spirit are tough they are also a very peaceful and full work for those who find its calling within them.

The mysteries are the binding constructs that 'govern' all of creation.

Magic, in its purest form, is the movement of the Power of creation. It is a divine movement of the Spirit of Creation that a practitioner may learn to create through their study.

To use magic to create imbalance is much like using a sacred, ceremonial object to kill another. The Spirit moves to Balance this action. In Eternity magic is sacred.

Medicine is the inherent Power existing in all things. All things have medicine.

The nature of creation is energetic. We are all expressions of coalescing energy.

Magic is sacred.

Life is magic

Prayer is a form of magic; magic is a form of prayer.

The works of Spirit, of magic, medicine, and mystery, compel their practitioners into movements. These 'movements' could also be called spells. The one who prays is casting a spell; a ritual is a spell that creates energetic movement; to dance the spirit is a spell. All movements of Spirit are energetic movements. The spiritual practitioner learns to create energetic movement.

A movement, a spell, is an energetic 'machine', or operation, that amplifies the energetic qualities of the intent behind it. A 'movement' is to turn a ripple into a wave, that the Spirit may move to work with us.

All things are energetic movements. A person who works on a project, regardless of it being spiritual, puts into its energetic qualities. Within the subtle realities the project is its own entity in a similar way to an energetic movement being its own entity. Each person working on a project includes their own energy. Each item or idea being used or applied includes its energy. Each value of every action applies to the Power of the energetic entity that is the project. All things are energetic movements. All things are 'spells'.

It is wise that a practitioner would build a relationship with the medicines, such as plants or crystals, they work with, coming to understand them in a personal way. A practitioner can then build on the medicines they work with if they choose.

Preparation is key in the works of Spirit. To prepare a spell in a precise way includes the Power of the work that went into preparing it. To prepare oneself for dancing a storm helps the practitioner catch the wind. To prepare oneself for the study of the mysteries opens the heart to revelation. Preparation is key in the works of Spirit.

The Spirit notices consistency in expression and gathers around that which is 'reinforced' in its intention. A sacred item or tool gains Power in this way through the accumulation of intent. The sacred tool then becomes its own Life, its own spirit. Many sacred objects, passed down through generations upon generations, carry with them the spirit of all who held them before.

The Spirit inhabits inherent Power, medicine, innately.

Traditional tools and sacred instruments are etched into the memory of creation. Their spirits live in the memory of Spirit.

All of creation is 'cyclical', circular. The binding constructs of Nature are paradoxical. The absolutes on the spectrum are not conflicted so much as extremities of a single principle. The Beginning and the End occur in the same place.

It is wise that a plant medicine person should seek first the medicines of the land they live on. Every land has medicines that apply to the ailments we often see. It is as though Creator and Mother Earth planned that each land should have its own plant medicines for its peoples. To work with the plant medicines of a land is also a great way to connect to its original spirit.

Meditation is a powerful tool in the magical practitioner's toolkit. To be able to meditate offers a practitioner the ability to work in the internal world, aligns their unconscious with their True Nature, and hone's their ability to enter the Sacred Silence that exists within all forms of spiritual trance.

There is a great Power in integrity. The practitioner of magical and spiritual works must maintain integrity. Integrity is among the things most valuable to Spirit. It is the good hearted people who know the works of Spirit best. The one who finds the fullness of their journey in Spirit is the one who learns to keep True integrity.

All things have their own energy. This energy is their spirit expressing through their body/mass. The spirit of a force, in any given moment, expresses through their body/mass creating an energetic texture. When a person refers to 'good vibes' they are saying that the energetic texture of the person, space, or thing is good.

All people naturally have an energetic sense. To experience the world through this sense is normal and natural. To develop it becomes a gift of Spirit. Each spiritual gift is equal parts burden and blessing.

As one learns to work with their energetic sense the sense expands, becoming greater. It is in this place where people begin to see auras and spirits.

Energetic sense is an instinctual sense that, within the unconscious processes, discerns the qualities of an energy. The energetic sense of a predator is much different than the sense of a sacred being. It is in a similar way that the energy of anger is not the energy of joy. Those with sight see the world through this sense. The unconscious processes of this sense integrate into the mind of the individual, creating a wider scope of potential information and a way of experiencing the unseen.

True sight can be a very overwhelming gift when it is not kept well. Sight demands a strong foundation. This foundation can be developed through many traditional wisdom teachings. Sight has the capacity to lead into madness. This gift must be given boundaries and kept with proper respect. To open sight without the wisdom to honor it and the equanimity to uphold it is likely to drive a person mad.

To uphold sight one must respect privacy, keep a mentality that is without judgment, and uphold integrity in their life.

To walk in the spirit world is to walk in our immediate energetic nature, our spirit and energy body. A person's immediate nature will form the energetic variables that designate what is attracted and repelled. The energetic state of a person will create the 'spirit world' they walk in. If a person who opens to the spirit world is keeping imbalance within themself, understanding that Spirit is the point of Supreme Balance, the energy and spirits that come to them will reflect this nature. To walk in the spirit world is to walk in the immediate energetic nature relating to the Spirit of Creation.

The entirety of that which exists within a person expands as they enter the spirit world. The small things become big things. That which was hidden is revealed and impacts the person's immediate relationship with Spirit.

A person's 'spirit world' intertwines with their environment. The environment of a practitioner becomes part of their spirit walk, impacting the energies and spirits that are attracted and repelled. One who walks in a temple will experience different spiritual realities then one who walks in a city. The one who walks in a temple will find their spirit walk to exist within the spirit of the temple. The one who walks in a city may find little structure to the Spirit and much toxic in the air.

A person who has sustained a spirit walk 'lifts up' their environment energetically.

To sustain a spirit walk a person must pass through their Personal Illusion.

A person must be healthy and 'clear' within their Nature to walk with the spirits in a good way. It is wise that a person should, before thinking to enter the spirit world, work towards a cleansing that brings them to the fullness of Self within their material form. One should not think to enter the spirit world until they no longer struggle to live well and uphold the fullness of Life.

Our soulful nature expresses within the spirit world, shaping our pathway. The one whose heart is good yet enters the spirit world in sickness will find that their path is shaped also by the goodness of their heart. The weight they bear will have become greater for having entered the spirit world in sickness, yet they will be guided by their heart as long as they remain steadfast.

To walk the spirit world expands potential. To expand upon imbalance creates great sickness; to expand upon Balance creates Spiritual Power and wisdom. Depending on the strength of the practitioner this expansion can either create significant illness or offer great wisdom and Power.

What the modern world calls 'medium' was once a traditional medicine that was given to mediate between the worlds of Spirit and Earth. The medicine person who would practice to speak with the spirits would mediate matters between the worlds and help to keep the balance of their community. The medicine person would be very gifted in their ability to speak with and hear the spirits.

Many beings watch over and guard Natural realities of creation in the spirit world.

The spirit world is the spirit of the physical world. It is a manifestation of the energetic realities of creation.

There are many places in the spirit world, many dimensions and planes. We may experience these worlds through visions and journeys, gaining insight into the workings of creation.

To walk the spirit world one needs the courage to rise above their fear. This courage is well found in a Faith grounded in innate Truth and universal Truth.

To walk the spirit world a person should seek good spirits who would help them and take part in their life.

The worlds of Spirit and Earth are meant to be aligned. As the physical world grew more distant from the Spirit we lost our connection with Spirit. As we lost this connection we lost much of the magic of life.

I spoke to a spirit of Nature who said: 'as the suffering of humanity grew worse their memory filled the space between our worlds. We shut ourselves away and forgot them for the spirit of their suffering, but our worlds are meant to be aligned.'

The spirit of Nature showed me, then, our worlds overlapping.

Our own being operates similarly to the energetic workings of creation. As we come to carry suffering, our suffering fills the space between our immediate state and our spirit. We forget into that loss and lose our ability to connect to Spirit. Within the world suffering fills a Universal Memory, creating an energetic resonance that rests between our immediate world and the spirit world. We, then, forget into the loss and lose our ability to connect to Spirit.

To each way of knowing there is a Spirit and within that Spirit exists the magic and medicine of the way of knowing. Spirit-Who-Moves-In-All forms around ways of knowing so They may relate to us. They take on the image of the way of knowing so that They may be known. Within the Spirit of a way of knowing exists the wisdom of the tradition.

Ancestral burdens and generational traumas affect our ability to sustain a walk in the spirit world. Before we step into a spirit walk we should seek to walk our healing journey and reconcile. To do this work also heals the spirit of our ancestors so that they may find their rest.

All of creation is conceptual mathematics. The values of all things come together as a cosmic equation, shaping the texture of reality. The unconscious thinks in conceptual mathematics.

"We are the key to The Temple."

Our unconscious is the key to The Temple. Who we are within our inner world is a key relating to The Temple of Eternity. The Temple opens its doors in accordance with this key in precise and Powerful ways. It is the movement of Spirit aligning with our immediate state. The one who has integrity within their inner-nature will have doors of The Temple open to them. The one without integrity will find these doors closed to them. To shape our inner-nature creates the key that unlocks The Way. Within this work we unlock the doors of The Temple that are within our Purpose.

Gratitude practices, such as counting blessings, are powerful manifestation techniques

The doors of The Temple remain closed except that one has worked to enter and sustain a spirit walk. A person who has not chosen a spirit walk should not expect to open the doors of The Temple. One may Know the blessings of peace in this world, carry wisdom, and walk in alignment with Spirit, yet the gifts of Spirit are within Their worlds. The mind of the one who has not learned to sustain a spirit walk is not open to the degree that allows them to experience and sustain the gifts of Spirit.

The entrance to The Temple exists within The Spirit World.

The energy of those who know Unity well repels spiritual predators. One who stands in Unity, which is integrity and Universal Truth, resonates an energy that predators cannot abide. It is to integrate a deep understanding of the value f Life. This resonance would also, over time, shape the physical life of the practitioner, repelling predatorial humans.

In all things, in every moment Grandfather Death exists, renewing them. Grandfather Death is the sacred shadow of Life.

Creator is the greatest of equations in the cosmic mathematics of creation.

There is a great Power in the actions we perceive as being 'small'. It is within the small actions that we create the means for great ones.

Magic, medicine, and the mysteries of creation are guarded by greater beings. Those who dabble, who do not transform to meet their Way, may find that recourse comes from the Spirit. The greater the practitioner's Knowledge the greater the expectation given to them by these greater beings.

Ones who do not honor the traditional teachings that they carry, in the way they are given to be kept, will likely find that there is repercussion within their life that comes through the Spirit. Greater beings watch over the traditional teachings and those who keep them.

It is wise to ask for help if needed in order to uphold the teachings. It is wise, even, if struggling, to ask for help to find the will to meet the expectations of the spirits and of Spirit.

The teachings we call esoteric were once considered sacred teachings to many cultures and traditions. Though their spirit has been forgotten in this modern world does not mean that they have become less sacred. It was once that only the 'priest/priestess', the medicine person, the devotee, was given to know the teachings we call esoteric. The work of learning esoteric knowledge, then, is the work of the devotee. To learn esoteric Knowledge should always be approached as a work of Spirit.

It is wise that a person should be conscious of and respectful towards traditional images and teachings. Traditional images and teachings carry with them the spirit of the tradition and the peoples who lived with and loved the tradition

Respect has a great Power in Spirit. Respect is magic. Respect brings things to Life.

The repercussions of Spirit appear as though fate itself had turned against a person.

Spirit, and the spirits, will seek to warn people about their actions before causing repercussion.

There are many worlds beyond our own and each is inhabited by spirits. We exist on an island at both the surface and the center of a great Ocean.

There are good spirits and there are bad spirits, much like there are good people and there are bad people.

It is wise that a person should seek to develop relationships with the spirits they work with. In this connection an understanding and mutual respect develops that helps clarify the spirit of the practitioner.

Discernment is required when working with spirits. Not all spirits are good spirits. We must understand the spirits we are working with in order to remain safe in The Spirit World. Those who do not work with discernment can cause damage to both themself and their environment.

The spirits are alive and they are sacred in their Life. They are not here to serve us nor do they exist to be studied. They are alive, much like humans are, existing within their own paradigm. Their life must be respected.

A practitioner should never bind spirits against the spirit's permission. A person seeking to empower an object or spell should instead create a relationship with the spirits they are seeking to work with. It is likely that an attempt to bind spirits would result in spiritual repercussions.

It is wise that a practitioner would never summon spirits. The spirits are alive. When we are seeking to commune with or work with a spirit it is wise that we should call them in, even if it takes many times calling. The good spirits see those who call with patience and persistence, keeping goodwill and discipline. Over time they would visit a person in the expectation of being respected properly for their presence, perhaps by lighting incense or giving good offerings. After calling them in a person should, then, build a relationship with them. The spirits will have expectations for the one calling them. The spirits are sacred beings who deserve to be respected as sacred.

To do one's spiritual work, act with integrity, transform to meet your Way, honor traditional wisdom teachings and values, and continue in learning pleases the spirits and greater beings. Through this work one may achieve their blessing.

It is wise that a person should call spirits in a structured way, honoring their life properly. It is wise that a person should never call in evil ones, for their gift is always toxic.

Spirit's names are sacred to them. It is wise not to use or share their names without permission being given from the spirit.

It can be difficult to hear a spirit's name being spoken. It is better to assume one does not know the name of a spirit than that they do.

The good spirits love those who give thanks for what they have.

The deities and spirits expect to be respected as sacred, not held as the only sacred force.

It is the Peaceful Warrior who succeeds in the works of Spirit. Balance is The Way.

There is a great Power in words. Words are magic. When we speak ill it is 'evil magic'. When we speak wellness it is 'Life magic'.

The dark paths in Spirit are not evil, rather they are a magic filled with very Powerful secrets that test those who seek them. In Unity all things must create and sustain Balance. The Sacred Heart of 'darkness' must also create and sustain Balance. The secrets within the darkness of Spirit test those who seek them to see if they are worthy. Those who fail are known to be driven mad or to become a predator. Were a practitioner to enter these paths without proper foundation, good practices, a steadfast spirit, wisdom, support, and guidance it becomes more likely they would falter. The consequence of turning towards this medicine and failing its test is suffering. Magic, in its purest form, seeks to create Balance for all life, regardless of dark or light. The secrets held within the darkness of Spirit offer to the practitioner their desires, forces them to face their fears, shows them their burdens and poisons, challenges them to overcome themself, etc... When a practitioner cannot remain poised in Balance, focused on wisdom, they become the monster that lives in the darkness within them. If they, in pursuit of this magic, remain poised in The Way, they gain a great Power and Knowledge that cannot be gained elsewhere. To think this Power is one that can be harnessed in pursuit of personal gain, however, is a sure sign of one who will fail the tests that live within the darkness of the Spirit.

Within the darkness live many beings that prey upon the weak of heart. It is the unwavering spirit, the Spiritual Warrior, that sustains The Way in these places. It is the Spiritual Warrior who turns away the predator, both within themself and in all worlds surrounding them, who succeeds in the paths that lead through the darkness.

A person may naturally journey during Sacred Silence, prayer, and meditation. This can feel like a powerful shifting of one's state of mind, a visioning, or as though one's spirit is traveling. This is a sacred occurrence that happens when Spirit communes with and moves a person. Medicine people tend to spend much time working with Spirit and so they learn to walk in these 'altered states'. To experience these powerful shifts was once considered natural, however has been forgotten by the modern world.

A person who journeys and receives visions should seek to return to an immediate, substantial understanding of reality. To return to your immediate reality 'completes the circle' of a journey or spiritual experience. If you experience a powerful shift it is wise to apply the following mechanism. If a person is not careful with these experiences parts of their mind and spirit may feel distant from their physical body. A good way to 'complete the circle' is to:

1. Follow the same path back that you took out as best able
2. Return to the Sacred Silence. Focus on the Sacred Silence
3. Observe your senses one by one. Observe taste, smell, hearing, feeling, and sight.

Through this small practice we may reconnect to a solid sense of reality. This practice helps our spirit find its way back to our body. When a person feels that their mind is still drifting after a meditation this practice can be applied to retrieve their mind and spirit from where it went.

It is wise that a practitioner would apply this same method as they both enter and exit a practice that includes journeying. It is to 'enter' and 'exit' the circle of a practice. To do this prepares the mind and spirit for its journey then returns the mind and spirit to its immediate life.

Traditional objects and tools, such as ancestral swords, have spirits that are their own. Traditional tools and their spirits have been passed down generations and deserve the same respect we would give to the wisdom keepers of our nation. The spirit of the sacred instrument may get angry at its keeper when not shown the proper respect. If we have taken on responsibility for a traditional tool we must respect it in the way it is given to be respected. This may mean that we must learn to become the image within us that respects them. It is well to ask for help in order to become the one within who respects them well.

Sex is not evil, nor is the primal essence innately destructive. These realities, often understood as 'impure', are Truly sacred aspects of creation. To not respect them as sacred, and in their sacredness, is to fall to their devices.

When a person uses a 'psychedelic' medicine, a big teacher, they bring their spirit into the spirit of the medicine. The state of the one seeking is brought into their relationship with the medicine. It is best to approach big teachers as great spirits and with the understanding that to use them is to commune with their spirit.

'Psychedelic' medicines, big teachers, can be approached with these three actions when you do not have access to traditional teachings and/or ceremony. They are: Clear Intent, Prayer, and Action

Clear Intent

One should have a clear idea of what they are seeking when using a big teacher. It is wise, also, to say it to the big teacher you are seeking to use. This acknowledges the spirit of the medicine and sets the intention for the journey.

Prayer

There is a spirit in the medicine that is very present and Powerful. The medicine and the journey should be approached as prayer and in prayer. They are sacred medicines that are 'prayer vehicles'. It is through their prayer that they teach us.

Action

One should always take at least one action back with them from a journey. This action anchors in the teachings received and honors the spirit of the medicine. It is wise that we should write down any action we seek to take. Even if we do not have the room in our life to take action it is appreciated that we acknowledge any guidance received.

The spirits of the big teachers love those who approach them with proper respect.

If a practitioner is using medicines it is wise to make known their purpose to the spirits and to Spirit. The deities, guides, helpers, etc… appreciate knowing that a person understands the purpose of the medicines they use. If a practitioner is using a medicine to cope with pain it is important to make known its necessity. If a person is using a medicine to teach them and guide them it is well to make this known. The spirits expect much from their medicine people and do not innately understand the use of medicines. When we make known how we feel and why we are using the medicine it helps them understand and gives them a chance to help.

In the works of Spirit it is better to master the simple and small action than to reach for the complex and great movement.

It is very easy for magic to become madness.

The Four Contributors to Energetic Movement

There are four main contributors to energetic movements, spells. The main contributors are: the state of the practitioner, the intent involved in the movement, the principles being applied to create movement, and the way of the movement itself.

"Magic expands upon the energetic state of its practitioner by the principles of its operation"

The state of being of the practitioner integrates with the magical operation to manifest the goal of the energetic movement. It is for this reason that to practice any form of magic or medicine is a way of life. The state of being of the practitioner becomes a part of the magic. The operation of magic is both a personal expression and a practical method. The one who does not keep their Balance as they practice will find that they manifest that which exists within their imbalance..

There are forms of magic that push against imbalance within a practitioner. These forms of magic may raise any underlying issues as the energy moves.

"Intent is the 'definition' of the energy channeled into an energetic movement"

Magical movements require that a practitioner learns to clarify and define their intent. Intent itself is the inherent definition of all energetic movement throughout all of creation. Intent is a force of Universal Consciousness. Should a practitioner not have clear and defined intent as they enter a magical operation the movement would also include the 'inconsistencies' within their intent. The definition of intent is often related to the state of a practitioner. A clear intent often creates a Powerful trance state, however when there are inconsistencies it is much more difficult for this trance state to be entered.

"The principles of the sacred objects, words, colors, symbols, tools, actions, astral alignments, spirits, sacred beings, etc... used for or called into a movement shape the qualities of the energetic movement"

The principles of an action or sacred object reflect and expand energetically within magical operation. Magic applies the medicine of actions and sacred objects, such as plants, to create energetic movement. The medicine of Cedar, as an example, is a strongly cleansing principle that aids in loosening deeply rooted imbalances. Cedar then, in a magical work or action, could be used to call in cleansing energies. An action's use is similar. To stand tall with one's back straight and shoulders raised creates an energy that reflects The Spiritual Warrior. Were a practitioner creating a magical movement then to 'stand tall' would bring in the principles of The Spiritual Warrior. Were a practitioner to light a candle, even, with intent the color of this candle would change the qualities of the energetic movement. The principles of an action, sacred object, tool, color, etc… expand within magical works, impacting the ripples of the movement.

The spirits and deities a practitioner may call into their works would shape the energies of their movements. The spirits and deities prefer that a practitioner gains their approval before calling them into a movement. They seek that a person should build a relationship and maintain a good way. If a person is not willing to do this it may be better to not call in spirits and deities.

It is important to understand the history of the sacred items being applied to the movement. Energy accumulates in accordance with intent. As an example, to use an object with a history of pain may inadvertently bring pain into the movement. If the object is to be used then one must work with its spirit and aid in cleansing the 'accumulated intent' which is the pain from its spirit.

"There are many ways within the Spirit. The 'operation' of our magic creates the movement of the energy"

There are many ways of moving energy that are 'magic'. The one who dances the Spirit, calling forth Power, operates magic. The one who prays and calls in the Spirit of Creation operates magic. The one who draws symbols and creates spells operates magic. The one who does yoga also operates magic. The movement of energy is defined by the way of our own practice.

These four main contributors play a role in all energetic movements.

All things are energetic movements.

The Seven Planes of Creation

Creation can be separated into seven fundamental 'planes'. These planes are: The Plane of The Elements, The Plane of The Plants, The Plane of The Animals, The Plane of The Meeting Point, The Plane of The Spirits, The Plane of The Demi-Urge', and The Plane of Gods and Goddesses.

The Plane of 'The Highest' is Unity. Unity is 'The Coming Together of All Things. They exist in all things as the essence of all things. Theirs are the principles of Oneness.

The Plane of The Elements is the first of the Natural Planes. The consciousness of the elemental spirits exists nearly outside of time. Their existence is harmonious with Nature's frequency. They are Unified Consciousness

The Plane of The Plants is the second of the Natural Planes. As Soul urges life to exist within creation, plants begin reaching for the light. They sing constant praises to the Spirit of Creation. Their song is also their Life. They are Directive Consciousness

The Plane of The Animals is the third of the Natural planes. It is the plane within which life begins to move within and around itself. The spirit of Life takes a more defined 'image', moving and learning within its environment. They are Reactive Consciousness

The Plane of the Meeting Point is the meeting of the planes of Spirit and Nature. At this point life begins to express 'complex consciousness' in matter. The meeting point is not solely humanity's. It is a plane for all beings who contemplate their own Nature and are gifted with co-creation within their material form. We are Complex-Reactive Consciousness. All Natural forces and beings have complex consciousness within the spirit world.

The Plane of the Spirits is the third of the Spiritual Planes. It is the plane where beings such as djinn, deities, and the spirits of Nature exist. They are Complex-Reactive Consciousness.

The Plane of the Demi-Urge' is the second of the Spiritual Planes. In this plane Natural forces take life and become spirits. This plane is of the arch-angels and the embodiments of Natural Forces. They are Complex-Directive Consciousness.

The Plane of the Gods and Goddesses is the first of the Spiritual Planes. It is the plane where gods and goddesses exist. They are Complex-Unified Consciousness.

The first of the Natural and Spiritual Planes are 1. The second of the Natural and Spiritual Planes are 2. The third of the Natural and Spiritual Planes are 3. The Meeting Point is both the fourth and the first.

The principles of 'Higher' planes take precedence over the principles of 'lower' energetically. The one who aligns their being with the principles of a 'Higher' plane will become able to move Power in ways that others cannot.

The words higher and lower do not fully represent the Nature of the planes within the Nature of Unity. The Nature of Unity is well understood through the principles of Oneness. The idea of greatness, then, is not applicable as one seeks to understand the Nature of the planes. 'The Highest' is beyond greatness. They are also the smallest.

Complex consciousness is a manifestation of consciousness that is marked by the gift of co-creation and the ability to contemplate ones own existence. Complex consciousness is of Spirit.

Consciousness is an essential building block of creation. Consciousness is an energetic field that allows creation to conceive of its own existence. Consciousness is that which allows for conception to occur.

The Personal Illusion

In order to walk The Spirit World a person must pass through their Personal Illusion. The Personal Illusion is a person's immediate unconscious state reflecting back to them as their 'dreamscape'. We all experience the world through our own 'illusion'. As a person enters a spirit walk their Personal Illusion grows in strength and fills their mind. As a person enters a spirit walk their Personal Illusion is capable of becoming the sole definition of their reality. A person who does not walk the spirit world can believe a thing without it taking them over. A person who has touched Spirit can have those beliefs become their only sense of reality. Our Personal Illusion is a dreamscape that is created through our unconscious state being reflected back to our conscious mind. A person who seeks the works of Spirit must pass through their Personal Illusion.

As a person seeks to pass through their Personal Illusion it is wise to adhere to these values: Awareness, Understanding, and Innate Truth

Awareness: We must step back into observation in order to see the Truth through the illusion. It is not that we must strive to see. It is, rather, that we must allow Truth to emerge.

Understanding: Seek to understand what is both within yourself and within the experience. Do not assume you know if you do not Truly. Understanding what is is also recognition of ignorance.

Innate Truth: One must adhere strongly to innate Truth in order to pass through their Personal Illusion. Innate Truth is well understood through embracing fact, the acknowledgement of ignorance, focusing on practical value, aligning with Self, and upholding the fullness of Life through the principles of Oneness.

A person who walks the spirit world well is clear and their Personal Illusion is well organized.

The Personal Illusion relates to The Four Worlds of Spirit energetically. We experience The Four Worlds of Spirit through our Personal Illusion until we learn to see beyond it. A person who *sees*, sees through their Personal Illusion.

The Four Worlds of Spirit

There are four 'Worlds' of Spirit. One may readily discern four energetic manifestations of the Spirit of Creation. They are energetic 'realms' that exist within Spirit. They are: The Spirit World, The Universal Memory, The Ocean of Spirit, and The Book of Life.

The Spirit World

There is a Spirit World within which the spirits live. They maintain creation, holding place within a great Temple. They watch over creation, helping to keep the Balance of that which is theirs. There are spirits in all things that are the energetic manifestation of the thing. A person who passes through their Personal Illusion steps into the domain of the spirits.

There are many domains in The Spirit World. Some of these domains include: The domain of the ancestors and the domain of the Natural spirits.

There are various spirit folk, each with their own way of knowing creation. The Spirit World is vast. It is as vast as the night sky, stretching in all directions.

A person who seeks to walk in The Worlds of Spirit must gain the approval of the good spirits and deities.

The Universal Memory

The Universal Memory is the memory of creation. The definition of energy, being energetic charge, imprints itself upon matter and creates a 'memory'. This relationship expands or contracts, becoming more or less subtle in relation to the material form. The stones are imprinted with subtle memory. The human form is given a less subtle memory. The Universal Memory is a product of the cohesion of energy. A room within which there was great joy will have joy painted on its walls. A room within which a person has endured suffering will have suffering caught on its walls. There is a memory in all things that is defined by the accumulation of energy. This action of creation pertains to Truth, being the complete definition of an energy. The sense of this memory can be subtle to the untrained eye, however is present to the extent that a person with a trained eye can watch the personality of another change as they enter a space. When a person enters a spirit walk they become attuned to the resonance of The Universal Memory. They become attuned to the subtle Truths of creation. They may perceive realities around them through the lens of the energetic memory of a space, translating through their Personal Illusion. The Universal Memory is the memory of creation. Energy, by the definition of its charge, imprints itself and defines the 'spirit' of a thing.

The Ocean of Spirit

We are all suspended within the energetic equilibrium of The Ocean of Spirit. All things are vibrations that resonate by their own principles and qualities. All things are as ripples within the 'pond' of their environment. Cedar, for instance, resonates a cleansing energy that is its medicine. It is this way for all things, expressing their spirit as energetic ripples in the pond of their environment. This is the Ocean of Spirit. A person who is angry ripples anger into their surroundings. A person who is joyful ripples joy into their surroundings. All things are suspended within an energetic equilibrium, resonating their qualities and principles.

The Law of Vibration: All things are vibration and resonate, subtly, their principles and qualities.

The Law of Harmonic Resonance: Vibration will seek to harmonize, except to adhere to that which is substantial.

The Law of Efficiency: Energy will seek its path of least resistance.

The Book of Life

Those who have entered into The Worlds of Spirit may perceive the workings of creation written in The Book of Life. All things are written in The Book of Life. The workings of creation are as energy lines, drawn in their own and holding their place. All things are written. One may discern a future that will come to pass within The Book of Life. One who can read The Book of Life is well aligned with the universal.

The Four Worlds of Spirit relate to each other naturally. The Universal Memory relates to The Ocean of Spirit. As energy resonates there is a subtle imprint caused within the Universal Memory. Times of great struggle create suffering that hangs in the air and blinds people to Truth. It is the relation of these two Worlds of Spirit. As suffering hangs in the air it sits between The Spirit World and a practitioner, defining, in a subtle way, the path of their spirit walk. The processes that govern these movements are held in The Book of Life.

The one who seeks to walk in the spirit world also walks within the memory of their environment. They become attuned to the Spirit of their surroundings through the memory of their environment. A person who upholds their spirit walk, then, challenges the memory of the world, 'lifting up' the energetic equilibrium of their surroundings through their alignment. The one who challenges the memory of the world in pursuit of Oneness heals the spirit of our world. As we enter into a spirit walk we become attuned to the memory of our surroundings. In this attunement we naturally challenge the memory of the world.

When we learn to enter and sustain a walk in the spirit world we may learn from the Spirit of a tradition. The old wise ones still live in that Spirit and would be glad for those who take their Good Work seriously to work with them.

The Five Fundamental Medicine Works

There are five fundamental medicine works that a person should seek to develop in order to sustain their spiritual, energetic, practice. They are: Sense, Knowledge, Intuition, Power, and Will and Intent.

Sense

Sense is the ability to discern energetic realities accurately. Sense and energetic discernment are fundamental to medicine work. The ability to sense accurately becomes an important part of maintaining stability in The Spirit World. A person who is proficient with sense will have creation 'speak' to them. They will understand what they are sensing intuitively as they continue in developing the ability.

To develop sense is to learn discern Truth through the personal illusion. This work begins with good observation, being a detached way of sight. As one works with sense they should always turn their eyes toward Truth, offering room for Truth to emerge through observation and detachment. This Truth is grounded in a tangible reality. One whose discernment reaches beyond what is wise has gone too far. In order to become proficient with sense one must be able to discern the nature of energy accurately. This ability comes through practice and observation.

As sense develops it integrates into other senses, opening the immediate being to experiencing energetic realities such as sight. A person who sees applies 'sense' through their sense of sight.

To develop sense it is important to become proficient with Sacred Silence, specifically developing ones capacity for Active Silence.

See: Practices and Prayers - Sacred Silence

To develop capacity for accurate sense a person should begin with practices that develop observation and detachment.

Observe your senses one by one. Taste, smell, hearing, feeling, and sight. Become accustomed to observing sense and attuning attention. It is wise that a person also is within the Sacred Silence as they practice observation.

Using the Sacred Silence, or in meditation, learn to detach from your immediate experience of reality. To 'take a step back' from your immediate understanding gives room for Truth to be observed. It is to look beyond one's self.

Over time, and if one is practicing, the practices of observation and detachment will aid in learning to discern the substantial Truth through energetic experience. These practices can also aid those already experiencing energetic realities in creating foundation with the gift. To return to a substantial and immediate Truth is a great way to structure any 'chaos' one may be sensing.

In the works of Spirit developing sense becomes the ability to remain stable in the spirit world. As one practices their ability to experience energetic realities tends to increase. It is for this reason that the ability to sense accurately relates to a practitioner's capacity for stability. To be able to sense with accuracy, being energetic discernment, helps keep the mind in a place of stability. To exercise one's capacity for accurate sense is to exercise one's capacity for stability in relation to experiencing Spirit.

We sense through our Personal Illusion. We must be able to discern Truth through the Personal Illusion in order to sustain sense.

One should not struggle to sense. Sensing occurs naturally and is as though seeing a thing. One need not wince to see what is in front of them. It is the same with sense.

In order to sustain sense there are principles that must be upheld by the practitioner. If these principles are not respected their gift is likely to become madness.

The principles that apply to sense are:

Privacy: When a person does not respect privacy their sense takes them too far and they become lost between the worlds. It is a natural occurrence. A person with sense, however, may see a thing that seems private. It is not their fault if they have not looked for it. In this instance return to yourself as though walking by a house you accidentally saw into through a window. It is a test relating to sense. The one who does not honor privacy as best able will find themself drawn into delusion.

Non-judgment: The person who cannot hold non-judgment with sense will find that their sense is filled with poison. They will perceive their judgments, and the suffering behind their judgments, instead of the Truth. They will also find that they become attached and can no longer perceive the Truth within the energy. They have decided what Truth is and so can no longer sense it. The one who works with sense must keep themself without judgment.

To practice with sense it is wise to begin with a sacred instrument

In order to work with sacred instruments, such as wands, staffs, and ceremonial tools, one must be aware of them energetically with accuracy. Developing one's sense is required of those who seek to work with sacred instruments. A person becomes connected to the instrument through their sense. The practitioner listens to it and learns from it. They tend to it's needs through sense. The sacred instrument will feel different if the instrument is not being well maintained. From this learning the practitioner grows in their practice. From this listening the practitioner learns to keep their medicine tool. The medicine tool, the sacred instrument, will tell a person when they are kept well and used well if the person has the sense to hear them.

To learn to sense sacred instruments, after having developed one's capacity for observation and detachment, is a good place to begin exercising one's capacity for sense.

Knowledge

There are two forms of knowledge that should be developed as one seeks to take part in the works of Spirit. They are substantial knowledge and energetic knowledge.

Our substantial knowledge is the direct knowledge of what we seek to work with. A person who seeks to work with plants would learn about the medicine of plants and how to work with them. They would develop knowledge of the plants that they use in their practice in a practical and tangible way. The one who seeks to practice dance magic would learn the steps they need to dance well. They would study the specific, tangible methods of dance. The one who seeks to exercise divination must find their method of divination and learn about applying it in a practical and substantial way. They must find their protocols and structures. To create this substantial knowledge in a practice grounds the energetic work so that the spirit does not fall out of alignment.

Our energetic knowledge is our knowledge relating to energy in general and to the energies of what we seek to work with.

Energy has its own Nature. Through developing energetic knowledge we create an understanding of why what we are working with works the way it does. We come to understand how to work with the energies, the spirit, of that which we seek to work with. A plant medicine person may develop knowledge relating how to commune with the spirits of the plants. A general understanding of how energy operates is an important action when seeking to work with the Spirit.

As we develop this general knowledge of energy we should also develop knowledge regarding the energetic nature, the spirit, of what we seek to work with. There are many various ways of moving and working with energy. All things are energetic movements, however when a person takes on the work of Spirit they learn to create energetic movement directly. A practitioner must come to understand the methods through which they may move and work with energy. A trickster should seek to develop their knowledge of how to strike the nuance. A dancer should come to understand the nature of the trance state, and other such actions of energy. One who practices divination may seek to develop their knowledge of how to commune with Spirit. To develop our knowledge of the method of working with energy that is directly related to our practice is necessary for the works of Spirit.

Spirit is in all things. The one who is taking part in the works of Spirit will find that, as their knowledge deepens, they innately learn to work with the spirit of their work. This occurs even in works that may be perceived as not specifically spiritual. The osteopath, for instance, who takes part in the works of Spirit may develop a medical intuition. The psychologist who integrates spiritual, energetic, knowledge into their practice will likely find that their mind becomes a thing of their own creation. Spirit is in all things. When we take part in the works of Spirit we deepen our connection to the spirit of our life and all that entails.

Our spirit expresses into life and guides us in our Way. What we seek to work with is our spirit expressing. As we seek to work with Spirit it is important that we understand that our work is also our Way. We are all called to different works. It is a part of our True Nature that we are called in our own Way. Our magic,our medicine, is an expression of our spirit.

All things have magic within them, not only the traditional works of Spirit.

Intuition

Intuition, as a fundamental medicine work, is the ability to step into and move in alignment with one's spirit. Intuition is the ability to move in alignment with that which is beyond conscious awareness. To move in alignment with that which is beyond conscious awareness is stabilized in Self-knowledge. Intuition, then, is a gate into the Self, one's spirit.

In the works of Spirit a person must be able to move in alignment with their spirit. They must be able to accurately intuit the Way that is theirs. To accurately intuit this Way is a gate that allows a person to become a spirit.

Intuition must be grounded in innate Truth. It must be grounded in fact, ignorance, practical value, the Self, and universal Truth.

There are two expressions of intuition. They are: The Movement of The Spirit and The Interconnection of The Soul

The work of intuition always begins in the movement of the spirit. In the movement of the spirit a person learns to move in alignment with their spirit through intuition. The fullness of intuition is sustained through and a gate into alignment with an individuals spirit. Through applying intuition toward aligning with the spirit behind the inner-knowing a person gains a powerful way to step into fullness. The movement of the spirit is the work of learning to walk as our spirit, our individual energetic expression, in this world. A person who has learned this alignment may find that they act in accordance with that which is beyond conscious awareness without conscious knowledge. Knowledge may come to them that they are meant to know. Many various things may occur that are expressions of intuition. These occur due to and in relation to the nature of their spirit.

To study the interconnection of the soul is a work of the devotee. It is a work of prophecy. One who studies the interconnection of the soul learns to pick up on the subtle impulses of creation.

To participate in the works of Spirit we must develop the intuitive ability to walk in our spirit's nature. It is for the reason of the works of Spirit existing within the energetic realities of creation that this is so. One who does not become a spirit has not Truly stepped into the works of Spirit. We must align with our own energetic expression. When we do it can feel as though we are walking in a flow that dances with the world around us. Coincidence may seem to dance with us. It is through an interconnection we cannot see with our eyes, yet perceive with our spirit. When we learn to align with our spirit's nature we align with the energetic existence of our life. Through this we gain the ability to move Power and to move Powerfully.

Those who have had past lives in the works of Spirit, who are predestined for spiritual work, who are raised in integrative wisdom teachings, or who have medicine people in their ancestry tend to be naturally more intuitive. They are naturally more connected to their spiritual nature so can be called intuitive. The connection to Spirit is more innate in these people. In this innate connection they have a stronger connection with their spirit. This connection then creates a natural intuitive ability.

There are three main actions one should take to develop the capacity for intuition. They are:

Integrate wisdom teachings and the understanding of universal principle deeply

To integrate wisdom teachings and the understanding of universal principle gives substance to the works of Spirit. The teachings must become as much a part of you as your own heart, This substance is necessary for crossing the bridge over to one's spirit. Through this work of learning intuition is given strong foundation.

Walk your Healing Journey and Reconcile

When we are unwell our spirit is unwell and we cannot Truly achieve the flow of intuition. We will not be able to walk in our spirit while keeping suffering. The suffering will infuse itself into our personal illusion and intuition will not flow properly.

Develop a substantial foundation in immediate reality relating to your True Nature

To have a foundation in your immediate reality that aligns with your True Nature, your Self, structures the flow of intuition. When we are seeking to develop intuition, to walk in our spirit, this foundation becomes a tether for our spirit.

Intuition will develop naturally if you take these three actions seriously.

If you seek intuitive ability it is wise to practice Sacred Silence, focusing on developing your capacity to keep Sacred Silence when active. Active Silence is a gate into the works of Spirit. To learn to maintain Sacred Silence while active opens the unconscious's ability to flow with creation. Active Silence, also, is likely to open spiritual, energetic, awareness. When the unconscious is offered more space to flow in relation room is created for intuitive ability. The unconscious becomes more able to act in alignment with that which is beyond conscious awareness through maintaining our connection with Sacred Silence and developing Active Silence.

Power

When a person studies Spirit Truly they gain an innate capacity for energetic movement. A person who Truly studies Spirit cannot help but to create Power. It is a deepening of the spirit within them that innately creates spiritual Power. As they come to Know they are made into one who sees. Through this Power comes to move through them regardless of their intent. When a person begins Truly working with Spirit it is necessary to understand the development of their Power. Capacity for energetic movement increases as one studies Spirit and becomes more proficient. It is necessary to understand the development of Power so that energetic, spiritual, injury is not created and the work is structured.

A person will innately develop the ability to move energy in the works of Spirit. If they are not aware of their Power and capacity for energetic movement the work can become confusing and dangerous.

The witch will be able to channel her will into her works. She may end up entering trance states as she practices. She may find that deities watch over her and move with her. She may find that spirits of Nature come to greet her, for the witch is well loved by the spirits of Nature.

If the witch doesn't come to understand her Power she may accidentally expand upon imbalance in a work. Her will, having grown, expands all medicines in a spell. Her will would then have to be met with more preparation and greater knowledge. The deities and spirits who come to know her and watch over her may, also, affect the world around her.

The medicine person may find that their will expands and becomes great. It may push against others without them knowing it. They may find that their medicine tools take on a Power and life of their own that innately affects other people.

If the medicine person doesn't come to understand the expansion of their will they may find that they accidentally hurt others. It is an energetic thing. The will, having grown and without yielding, pushes against the space of others. If the medicine person lets someone who isn't ready use their sacred instrument they may accidentally injure the person energetically.

The mystic may find that the world moves around them in accordance with their innate energy. It is Truth. They 'lift up' the world. They may experience moments of great clarity and visions that guide them. They may find Spirit moving through them to accomplish things in the world.

If the mystic doesn't acknowledge where they are they may accidentally bring another into a place they are not ready to be in solely because they 'lift up' the world. They may be confused with their visions, moments of clarity, and the movement of Spirit reaching through them. Others may receive visions around them.

When a person studies Spirit Truly they cannot help but to create Power. When a person does not understand their Power, and the nature of their Power, they can create imbalance. As a person grows in Spirit the small imbalance is capable of creating significant repercussions.

Will and Intent

Our will is an expression of our life-force. Its definition is called Intent. When we approach the works of Spirit we must learn to apply our will and clarify our intent. Will and Intent are energetic forces that relate to our ability to move the world around us and remain stable in The Spirit World.

There are three forms of will. They are:

The will's channel: The will's channel is our immediate being. It is the channel willpower, life-force, takes as it expresses into life. The will is our energetic force and it expresses through the vehicle of our being. Our being is programmed by the will and intent to be this channel.

The will to overcome: the will to overcome expresses from our soul and is applied through our consciousness. The will to overcome is our conscious ability to overcome our will's channel and create of our unconscious. As we exercise our will to overcome we exercise our conscious connection with our soul and clarify our intent. The will to overcome is best applied to create changes in the will's channel. To work with medicine will requires that we have clarity within our will's channel.

The Medicine Will: The medicine will is the will of magic and spiritual medicine. It is a deep Power existing in all people that is capable of directly affecting the energetic nature of creation. Medicine people and spiritual practitioners are capable of working with and moving medicine will. To work with and move medicine will opens the mind and turns a person into a spirit.

To exercise our will to overcome and create our channel in the image of our True Nature is the work of will. This work liberates The Medicine Will. One may begin this work at any time simply by accessing their will to overcome in pursuit of becoming their Self or acting to change their unconscious being. One may build their channel by challenging thoughts, working with emotions, exercising, developing their connection with their True Nature, etc…

Intent is the definition of willpower. As will proceeds forward, intent gives it definition for its movement. The body intends that the heart should beat so it does. The mind intends that a thought should happen so it does. The innocence intends that one should feel so we do. Intent is the definition of energetic movement, being willpower.

When we seek to work with Spiritual Power we must be adept with our Intent. We must clarify our intent. That clarity is alignment with our spirit. The works of Spirit are Powerful and when our intent is not clear it can create inconsistencies in our energetic movement. To be adept with intent is to be able to clarify our intent. This 'clarity' can come in many forms. One may prepare for an energetic movement through clarifying intent. One may empty themself into equanimity that the Spirit may clarify their Way. One may build to reach the will of the warrior, being the ability to hold one's ground without doubt. The goal is to be able to clarify one's intent so there are no inconsistencies as one approaches the use of Spiritual Power. .

It is wise to understand that one is accessing a space that could be called 'intent without doubt' as they create energetic movement. It does not necessarily mean that there is no doubt so much as that one has entered the mind that is without doubt.

Clarity of intent accompanies the True Nature's expression

Will and Intent are universal forces. As Creator manifested Themself as creation it was Their will that made it so and Their intent to do so. At a fundamental energetic level the force of all things is Creator's will moving as life-force. At a fundamental energetic level all movement in creation is directed by Creator's intent.

The Darkness of Peace

Peace is a choice
The heart chooses of its own volition
The darkness of the heart is often stronger than its will to surrender to The Way
It is suffering; it is an addiction to pain
We must liberate the heart
For in peace there is a vast darkness to remember

I once questioned my primal fire, my animal spirit
saying; 'are you the evil they speak of,
which solely consumes?'
My animal spirit spoke,
saying: 'I am trapped
and because I am trapped I am rage.
Sit with me and show me The Way
And I will live in you...
Until I know Life I cannot Live.'
Then the Spirit took me
They showed me that Balance is more of the animal than of the human who has forgotten their Nature
We have forgotten our humanity as we locked away our Nature
Urged to dominate Her forces, ourselves
We called it evil to be as One with the Nature that conceived us
Body and Soul
Animal and Spirit
Earth and Fire
Not one without the other, but both as One

In the game of mind's the warrior fights with words
Reaching their goals strategically
Contemplating the field of battle
Adapting to their environment
This my animal spirit revealed as I sat with him
That in him I am not bound to the ways of the forest
For Nature is more than what conceived of us

My instincts are not bear or crow or wolf
They are human!
In liberation the spirit in me saw
as I fell
that Life lives in the Balance of All
and All lives in the Balance of I
Liberation, thought my Silence,
Is deep recognition,
Is Balance in all that is me
Is learning The Way

Peace is a choice
My heart whispers when sitting in my animal spirit
Of readiness to attain, of a want to Live!
For when the darkness cleared and freedom was returned to that place, my animal spirit
My Silence spoke of passion and Balance, seeking to understand life and its great potential
I am the animal who seeks to know, I am curiosity
That is where I seek, in my animal spirit I contemplate
Driven by an urge to Live and rejoice
and driven to Live by the urge to learn and create
Knowing I am an animal of Spirit
An expression of Balance

The urge rose from within my soul
When I was beneath the deep shadow of my past
It burst into a twin flame
The spirit and the animal
The fire and the earth
The Thought and the Life
Neither more than the other
Both fulfilled by the other
As I fell I saw this great thing
And it drove me to rise up, like Nature Herself had called me

Peace is a choice
Peace is the liberation of the heart,
The coming to peace with our darkness
That we may be revealed and reveal our Self as Life
Even those which we have called dark and seen with fear
Are keepers of our Way
In our darkest depths there is a part of our Truth that calls for help
We have forgotten, even there,
For in that entrapment there is a pain that knows poison well
We call for unconditional love and understanding, waiting to be seen
Life is our healing journey
It is Truth that knows Balance; it is Delusion that believes it knows better
It is the entrapment, the delusion, in which we say 'good or evil'
It is not so
There are those who seek to Live and those who do not know how

Nothing is 'wrong' solely because it is
Neither is it 'wrong' solely because we are told it is
My animal spirit, who is Jaguar Crow,
Keeps my Way as I keep him and we are One
My animal spirit guides me to fulfillment, keeping my Balance
Reminding me of a great passion for Life
To walk the shadow of self, keeping The Way, is to find the light within
To walk the light of self, keeping The Way, is to find the shadow within
All that's left is to Live
This is the darkness of peace

The peace of the primal is also the peace of the divine
Intertwined in a twin flame, inseparable except to divide
In eternal conflict,
Yet the dark does not war with the light,

Neither does the light war with the dark
The eternal conflict is the conflict itself
The liberation of the heart's darkness is peace
And it is to reveal what was hidden as Life manifesting
I saw in the animal spirit a great Light, and it is also the Light
that shines from the Spirit
Balance is The Way

The Stand

We are the ones who stand for the soul of the world
While the consumed consume it
And the ones who stand above watch on, perverting their essence
We are the ones who tend the Fire,
Raising the torch high
To light The Way

We are the ones who see
In all things Balance
The Sacred Heart of creation beating within All
The blades of grass enlightened
The beggar's wisdom,
The lord's folly
And calling out the suffering
That we may challenge our self to see

We are the ones who stand for the soul of the Earth
As the blind ravage Her body
And the ones who do not Know are consumed in a quest for more
We are the ones who tend the Fire,
Raising the torch high
To light The Way

We are the ones who see the past repeating
The undefeated
Saying 'this cannot continue!'
'This cannot happen again!'
Watching the children drown themself in The Stream
For the folly of the world
We are the ones who say:
'Balance is The Way and it has many paths'
In the search for more we have forgotten what we have

For in the beating heart of every person
Lives a great revelation
It is that Life is The Way
In scriptures, in stories, in teachings
These things have been spoken countless times
By elders, by masters, by teachers, by sages and yogis, by
Buddhas, by priests, imams, and rabis
Yet we listened to the ones who did not Know
For their words were coated in sugar
And sweet as honey,
Truth is bittersweet!
We became sick, humanity
Then stole the Life of others for our greed

We are the ones who stand for the soul of the world
The True warriors
We are the ones who tend the Fire
Raising the torch high
To light The Way

We are the ones who stand for the soul of the world
The ones who stood when all seemed lost
The ones who continued on when the weakness came
And brought us to our knees
We are the ones who tend the Fire
Raising the torch high
To light The Way

We are the ones, among many,
Not the taught, yet often so
We are the ones who stand
Hearing Truth, and saying: 'This cannot continue'
We are the living and the others are dead
Yet in this age the dead may rise again
For Life is more than suffering
So sit at the fire we have tended for generations

keeping it against the predators who sought to smother our flame
You are welcome here
And in the light see visions of the horrors inflicted
The revelation of peace beyond this work
The work of reconciliation
We have carried your weight,
The spiritual warriors of many ages
That there may still be Light in this world
As we, humanity, are offered a chance
To surpass the darkness that consumed us

This age condemns itself
For its power and knowledge
Misunderstanding the Nature of creation
And believing itself beyond reproach
Truth will not compromise
It will not bend or yield
This age will end
And the Fire will remain
Lighting The Way
The spirits of those who stood
Dancing 'round it
Rejoicing,
For it is we who found Heaven

Blindness can never see the Truth
Ignorance cannot Know the Truth
Poison cannot abide the Truth
Consumption cannot ease the Truth
And suffering cannot sustain
The choice remains to surpass the Lie
It is for the stand of the spiritual warriors that this choice remains
Those who stood when the weakness came and brought them to their knees
As the world condemned them for the Truth they kept
The Fire they tended

That we are given this chance

We are the ones who stand for the soul of the world
The spiritual warriors who stand with humility
Embracing Truth, and saying: 'this cannot continue!"
We are the ones who tend the Fire
Raising the torch high
To light The Way

We have chosen this journey, this stand
And the choice remains for every person
So take The Stand
Join us at the Fire we have kept
You are welcome here

Practices and Prayers

Higher Powers

For those who may be seeking an understanding of 'Higher Power', or a clearer understanding of their own Higher Power, I offer the teachings I have received. I feel it is important to offer this understanding that others may find within themself what is their own understanding. Spirit is a Way with many paths.

Creator

Creator, The-One-Who-Conceived-Of-All, is life itself. The big bang was Their out-breath. Before the beginning They existed, and past the end They exist. All things exist within Them. Through Them all things come to Life and are given to Live. They conceived of Themself as life so life came to exist. They have had many names throughout creation. With each They are also the Creator. They are The Hidden One, guiding The Way, for all things are Theirs even when left nameless. They are the humility of the ant and the majesty of the mountain. They are the divinity of both man and woman; the strength of The Divine Masculine and the fortitude of The Divine Feminine. They are the people; the elements, plants, and animals. They are the first breath of Life and the final passage of Death. They are the Unity which is above, within, and below all of creation. The Nature of Creation is Their Nature expressed. Within Them all is conceived, for all is conceived of Them and it is through Them that creation exists. They are all things coming to fullness. They are Jah, Wakan Tanka, Allah, Yah Weh. GOD, etc… Creation is Their body. Everything in creation is a self-reflection of Creator. All is an expression of Them. All things are expressions of Them. They are that which is beyond knowing for They are all Knowledge. They are the interconnection of Love; the destruction of pride; the will of the wise; the peace of the True. The Nature of all things is Their movement. They are Creator, Whose Life is hidden behind, within, above, below, coming through All and is All.

Unity is a name of Creator. Unity means: 'The Coming Together of All Things'. All things return to Oneness in their most essential nature. As all things return to Oneness they pass outside of time, returning to origin. Within origin all things are all things in Oneness. It is 'The Beginning and The End' existting as the essence of all things. This Oneness that is All-Things is Unity. Unity is 'The Coming Together of All Things'

Spirit-Who-Moves-In-All

There is a Spirit that moves in and through all things. They are the Spirit of Creator, the Spirit of Creation. They are the energetic manifestation of creation. They are the expression of Life expressing in life. As All conceives of Themself Their Spirit forms, moving in and through all things. They weave into the fabric of creation as the fabric of creation. It is Spirit. Every thing is given its spirit through this. This is the formation of Spirit, that each thing may express its nature energetically. Spirit, also, is the reach of Creator seeking to return to Their Nature. Spirit is a river called Truth; a current carrying us Home. In all things Spirit is a web of intersecting currents harmonizing within the moment. Spirit is the calling within us. Spirit is our calling, for Theirs is the fullness of Life. Spirit moves within all things as the energetic manifestation of creation. They are a deep current calling us to the fullness of Life.

Mother Earth

We are all children of Mother Earth. She is part of our essence. Our spirit is an expression of our Mother's and all our relations across Her body are our family. We are One with Her. The trees sing a constant prayer song to The Divine. We have this same song within us. It is our Nature. It is to sing the song of our Life. Our bones are her bones; our blood is her blood; our heart is her heart. Her elements are our body; her water is our water; her air is our breath. When we are connected with our Nature we are also connected with Her. Her song lives in us and through us. We are all children of Mother Earth.

Mother Earth has a spirit of Her own. She is much like a goddess. We are all Her children and part of Her body. She loves those who seek to know Her well.

To connect to the spirit of Mother Earth see: Practices and Prayers - The Oneness Prayer

Sacred Silence

Sacred Silence is a teaching from Grandfather Stalking Wolf, an Apache scout and spirit walker through his apprentice Tom Brown Jr. from the book Awakening Spirits.

Sacred Silence is a meditative Silence that exists within all forms of spiritual trance. Sacred Silence is the vehicle of spiritual trances. Prayer, meditation, gnosis, trance, etc… are shapes the Sacred Silence takes while the Sacred Silence is the vehicle that allows them to accomplish their movement.

Sacred Silence is the vehicle of spiritual, energetic, movement. To develop your connection with Sacred Silence, regardless of the method of practice, is to develop your capacity for energetic, spiritual, movement. As a person enters Sacred Silence their spiritual, energetic, forms are freed to move. The consciousness releases the hold on the unconscious so that the unconscious may move and realign. The spirit, in this release, is freed to move and journey. Regardless of the method practiced, entering the Sacred Silence is to create room for the energetic realities of our being to move.

The 'thought' of the original essence, the soul, is kept in Sacred Silence. When we practice to connect with Sacred Silence, in its various forms, we increase our connection with our soul. We offer space for our soulful directive to flow freely within us. A person, even, may find Sacred Silence to come to them during activities and actions that are aligned with their soul's nature. A person, for instance, who loves dancing may enter a flow state while dancing. This is because the 'thought' of the soul is kept within the Sacred Silence. As that person is aligned with their soul's nature they deepen their connection with the Sacred Silence through the action that is connected to their soul's nature. The 'thought' of our soul is kept within the Sacred Silence so there is a natural connection that exists between the Sacred Silence and the soul. Actions that are aligned with our soul's nature are, for this reason, prayer. They are actions that bring us closer to that which we are given to be.

Sacred Silence is its own energetic force within creation. One can hear the Sacred Silence in the trees if they know how to listen. When we practice Sacred Silence we connect to that innate energetic force within our immediate existence. We connect to that universal energetic force and cultivate our connection with it. Through this we exercise our connection with that which the energetic force is connected to within our immediate existence.

Sacred Silence is a powerful tool for creating a healthy and full life. Within Sacred Silence exists various direct benefits. It is, even, that Sacred Silence, in its various forms and even without a name, is an important part of maintaining a healthy lifestyle from an integrative viewpoint. When we enter Sacred Silence we offer room for our unconscious to reorient on the fullness of our life. We release the attachments that hold our unconscious in a shape that is not full. One who cultivates their relationship with Sacred Silence must release these attachments to maintain that relationship. Sacred Silence is a powerful tool for creating a full life.

When we cultivate and maintain our connection with Sacred Silence it helps mark the fullness of our life. A person who practices Sacred Silence will find that the issues that keep them away from fullness appear to them while they are practicing. It is for this reason that cultivating and maintaining one's connection with Sacred Silence is a good marker along our path to fullness. A person who practices Sacred Silence will find that they begin challenging the items that exist within their unconscious that keep them away from good living.

Sacred Silence is a tool that anyone and everyone may use to work with their unconscious and with Spirit. A person who develops their connection with Sacred Silence gathers a tool within their life that they can use to work with and check in on themself. At any point, when a person has practiced Sacred Silence, they may take a moment and check in on themself. It is a very valuable tool.

Sacred Silence is a very important practice in The Way of Unity. A person who seeks to practice what is offered within The Way of Unity should seek to cultivate and maintain their relationship with Sacred Silence. Sacred Silence is the substance of all the practices offered in The Way of Unity.

Method

Apply steps 2-6 as needed. Be conscious of what works for you.

1. Be Still

It is wise to begin with stillness, laying down or in easy pose. Once practiced one may proceed to bringing Sacred Silence into activities.

2. Relax

Relaxation practices are very important when seeking to practice Sacred Silence. A useful relaxation practice is to consciously go to tension and intend to relax, envisioning the muscle relaxing and feeling that relaxation deepen. This step is very important. Without relaxation a person cannot reach the Sacred Silence. If you are struggling to relax it is wise to apply deeper relaxation techniques, such as taking a bath or yoga, prior to practicing Sacred Silence.

3. Let Go/Detach

Intend to let go. Let go of what is within you and let it move. In order to enter Sacred Silence you must release. Through letting go your thoughts will become able to move in a way that allows you to enter Sacred Silence.

4. Become Aware of Your Being, Connect to Your Being

Take a moment to listen and be aware of your immediate being. In the relaxation, just listen and be aware. Let it connect you to yourself. As things rise let them pass. Do not attach to them. Do not be concerned with them. If they begin racing, ask your mind, in your thoughts or out loud, to give you space to practice Sacred Silence. Say: 'I will come to you later when I feel more able' and 'the Sacred Silence will help me work with you'. Then you must also return later and work with your unconscious. Return to relaxation and letting go if necessary.

5. Focus on your Breathe

Focus on your breathe while relaxing and letting go. Allow it to deepen your relaxation and help you reach the Sacred Silence. Breathe in a way that is comfortable for you or in a way that brings you comfort.

6. **Envision Sacred Silence while Relaxing**

Envisioning offers the unconscious a viable focal point. Senses and images are the way the unconscious speaks and listens. To envision a meditative Silence offers the unconscious a way of understanding where you are seeking to go.

Relaxation and letting go will also bring one to the Sacred Silence, however to teach the unconscious to listen to the vision creates a more versatile exercise. If you do not have a vision of Sacred Silence it is wise to focus on the relaxation, letting go, and listening until you have a sense of the Sacred Silence.

7. Work with your Thoughts to Move Towards Silence

Work with your thoughts as you move towards the Sacred Silence. Remain detached as best able. Apply the previous steps as they are needed. Relax and let go and let your thoughts move, gently returning your focus to the Sacred Silence. It is a pathway. As you become more proficient with Sacred Silence this step will become easier. As it becomes easier you will also find that your mind is more capable of maintaining its connection with the Silence outside of the practice.

8. Be within the Sacred Silence

When you have reached the Sacred Silence be in the Sacred Silence. If you have applied envisioning Sacred Silence, release the vision. Rest within the Sacred Silence.

The Sacred Silence is a vehicle through which you may work with your unconscious. You may find, as you become more accustomed to the Sacred Silence, that your unconscious uses the space to try to work with you, bringing items to the surface of your mind so that you may sit with them.

9. Return to Immediate Life

Before leaving the practice, observe your five senses briefly. Observe taste, smell, hearing, feeling, and sight. Do your best to keep the Sacred Silence as you observe.

10. Give Thanks

Sacred Silence and The Unconscious

One cannot accomplish energetic works without the Sacred Silence. Our unconscious is an energy form within us. Without Sacred Silence the unconscious cannot move and reorient. Without Sacred Silence one would struggle to heal their unconscious. It is because the vehicle for that movement is Sacred Silence. Without Sacred Silence we do not offer our unconscious the means to create movement within itself.

Sacred Silence is a powerful way to work with our unconscious. A person who has a daily practice of Sacred Silence would find their quality of life to be markedly improved. Within the Sacred Silence a person will find that:

1. They create the space to sit with their unconscious
2. The unconscious may shift, reorienting itself
3. A person may have spiritual experiences

Sacred Silence offers room so a person may sit with their unconscious.

When a person enters Sacred Silence their unconscious may take the opportunity to share what they are experiencing beneath the surface. This is a great opportunity to work with our unconscious and create a better life. A person may find that their unconscious communicates with them to gain conscious guidance on what they are carrying. The unconscious can take many shapes in this communication. It may bring emotions to the surface. It may speak through the little selves, younger versions of yourself, so a person can understand what they are experiencing. It may bring thoughts to the surface so a person can work with them and challenge them. When a person enters the Sacred Silence they enter a space where they may sit with their unconscious and overcome what they are struggling with. This space, then, is a powerful tool to help us realign with the fullness of our life.

Within the Sacred Silence the unconscious may shift, moving pieces of itself.

When a person enters Sacred Silence they offer room for their unconscious to reorient. When the conscious mind releases its attachment, the unconscious is freed to move. This is a great key to alignment. Sacred Silence is a vehicle for this movement. The unconscious, as it is able, will shift to uphold a person's life. It will enact this shifting except that it meets blocks. These blocks, then, will likely be communicated to a person who is consistent in their practice. If a person doesn't meet their 'blocks' with wisdom they will find that their practice becomes limited.

Within Sacred Silence the spirit of a person may journey.

When a person enters Sacred Silence it is a place where Spirit may communicate with them. A person may have spiritual experiences when they enter Sacred Silence. This is called a journey. Journeys are a natural and normal part of life when we are living in alignment with the fullness of our existence as humans. It is unlikely journeys will occur frequently, however the space of Sacred Silence offers room for them to occur. When a person experiences a journey it is wise to understand that they must return to the Sacred Silence, 'complete the circle', before returning to their life. The path we take out is the path we must take back.

Completing The Circle

When we enter a journey in Sacred Silence it is important that we remember to complete the circle. To complete the circle we must come back to our immediate life before returning to our immediate life. When we go on a journey our spirit, our energetic being, has gone somewhere within the infinite Consciousness of creation. When we do not come back we can leave that part of us where we went. It can feel as though we are distant from ourself when we do not complete the circle of a practice. It is because we would have left our spirit somewhere other than where we are.

To complete the circle:

1. Take the Same Path Back That You Took Out

A person should do their best to follow back the same path that they took out. This principle is not always direct, however it is proper form when journeying.

2. Return to Sacred Silence

Before returning to your immediate life, briefly focus on returning to the Sacred Silence. The Sacred Silence is your landing platform and the vehicle that allows you to travel. When you do not return to Sacred Silence you may struggle to 'land'.

3. Apply a Grounding Technique

After returning to the Sacred Silence apply a grounding technique that helps you reorient on your immediate life. A good grounding technique is to briefly turn your focus towards your five senses. Move through taste, smell, sight, hearing, and feeling.

4. Return to Immediate Life

After applying the grounding technique you can return to your immediate life without leaving pieces of your spirit behind. It is also wise to give thanks.

Water Cleansing Prayer

A cleansing practice is a fundamental spiritual practice. It is an important and sacred action within many traditions. In this work I offer a 'Water Cleansing' prayer to any and all people seeking to develop a stronger connection with Spirit. The Water Cleansing has no doctrine and is a way that anyone may cleanse their spirit.

To apply a spiritual cleansing practice is to wash our spirit. Our spirit is our energetic being and is the home of our individuality. A clear sense of individuality is a healthy spirit and it is innately interconnected with creation. The principles of our spirit, then, are individuality and interconnection. Within this, it is important to understand that the spirit is not specifically spiritual, rather it is the home of our individuality and interconnection.

To apply a spiritual cleansing practice is to wash our spirit. Much like our body gathering dirt throughout the day, our spirit may accumulate energetic resonance that clouds its clarity. We take a shower to clean our body so we do not grow ill. We apply a spiritual cleansing practice so our spirit does not grow distant. To 'wash' our spirit is to release the accumulated energetic resonance we may have gathered throughout our day.

A spiritual cleansing practice is a great tool to use when needing to calm yourself.

A spiritual cleansing practice is one of the most important tools in the spiritual practitioner's toolkit. The spiritual cleansing practice becomes a fundamental, easily applied method to maintain spiritual clarity.

Method

The Water Cleanse is a prayer within which we ask the spirit of Water, and our Higher Power/s, to cleanse us energetically. It is wise, in this, that one should understand that Water is alive. Water's spirit carries their medicine and when applying this prayer we are asking the Water's spirit for this cleansing.

1. Step into Sacred Silence Near Water

Having water nearby, such as at a running faucet, ask for help to cleanse your spirit. Do your best to be in a calm state of mind. Ask the spirit of Water to cleanse you. Ask, also, those who you may feel connected to. Do your best that the prayer should be heartfelt and spoken from the Sacred Silence, a calm state of mind. I offer my own words and Truth to those who need it. If you are struggling to find the words you may use:

Please, Spirit of Water
Please Creator, Mother Earth, Spirit-Who-Moves-In-All
Cleanse my spirit and help me stand in my True Nature

2. Bring the Water Over Your Body

While speaking the prayer, or after speaking it, wash your body. Begin with hands and forearms making sure to get the crook of your elbows. Bring the water to your face. Briefly wash your hair, behind the ears, the back of your neck, over the top of your head, and anywhere else you feel you may need cleansing. It is good, after washing the forearms and head, to brush the water down both the front and the back of your entire body. Bring the water to anywhere you may feel your spirit calling to be washed.

Using The Water Cleanse in a shower is a great way to prepare for a day energetically. If cleansing in a shower make sure the water touches every single part of your body while you are cleansing. This separates the Water Cleanse from regular showers. This action includes cleansing between the toes, behind the knees, one's private parts, and the armpits.

3 **Give Thanks**

After finishing the Water Cleansing give thanks to the spirit of Water and to Creator. Give thanks for the help you have received and continue in good works.

Holding Space

(This practice is a way of creating and holding Sacred Space, a practice gifted to me from Sami teachings)

Holding Space is a practice of learning to hold an energetic space around one's self. Holding Space is a great way to create safe space energetically and to learn to stand in one's Power. When a person learns to hold space ably they become able to maintain their energies to the degree that predators and predatorial energies cannot feed from them. Holding Space creates an energetic push against predators, both in the spirit world and the physical world. This work, of learning to hold space, teaches us to stand as the spiritual warrior and hold a space for healing. Through it we may help our being learn to hold our ground and come to a greater sense of peace in our life.

This practice is a fundamental work for those who seek the works of Spirit. A person should do their best to become adept with this practice before entering the spirit world.

Method

1. Enter Sacred Silence

It is wise to become proficient with Sacred Silence prior to practicing Holding Space. In order to practice Holding Space Sacred Silence is necessary. It is the graceful touch that holds the greatest Power in Spirit.

2. Become Self-Aware; Connect to Yourself

Turn your mind's eye inward. Listen to your being and let it connect you to yourself..

3. Envision a Light Shining from Your Innermost Truth, Filling the Orb of your Spiritual Space

Envision a light shining from your innermost Truth. See the light surrounding you and filling your orb. It is a gentle light, shining and filling your orb. Your original essence is a lantern shining this light that fills your orb. This light doesn't push against anything. You don't need to push to shine it. It is shining, warming and comforting you, creating a space for you. Be in the light. See it; feel it; rest in it. Sit in the light and let it comfort you.

4. Find Rest in The Light

Do your best to find rest in that light. To find this rest helps to keep the Sacred Silence and the graceful touch.

Feel that this space is a safe place. Let it be a place where you can rest. Let it be a sacred space. Finding the sense of it being a safe space helps make it a safe space. It offers you a place to return to. To know it is a safe space is important for it to become one.

5. Once you are able to rest in the light you may approach the following optional steps.

(optional) Connect to the Stance of The Spiritual Warrior

When you feel ready, and find a sense of peace in the light, connect to the stance of the Spiritual Warrior. The spiritual warrior exists in us all. It is the part of us that is stone flowing like water. Let your spirit strengthen in this space, shining the light and finding rest within it. Do this in a gentle way, staying in the light. Learn to hold your Power within your sacred space. Over time the holding of this stance will help you maintain your innate Power.

(Optional) Envision Barriers Surrounding your Orb of Light, stopping destructive energies from entering and/or taking away from you

Over time, and as you feel able, envision barriers surrounding you, protecting you. Envisioning a wall works well to create these barriers. These barriers surround your orb so that destructive energies cannot pass through. These barriers will help strengthen your spirit against predators. The light will push them away and keep you strong. The barriers will stop them from even being able to reach you. These barriers are a peaceful expression of the Spiritual Warrior. They are an armor we can use if the need is ever called for.

These barriers can also be used to create energetic barriers that can help empaths and other sensitive people from feeling what isn't theirs. If you place a barrier consistently it becomes an energetic barrier in your unconscious.

One may also use outward facing mirrors in place of the barriers. The reflective principles help to repel destructive energies. If you feel like destructive energy is being turned toward you and you have practiced enough, you can use a mirror to reflect the energy back to the one who is sending it. It takes less effort to use the mirrors when defending ones self energetically than it does to use barriers.

(Optional) Use the Space to Heal and Grow

This space, filled with light and rest, comforting your being, is a space that can be used to heal and do inner-work once you become proficient in its practice. To find this sacred space becomes a place where we may help our unconscious heal and grow. Holding Space can be a way of connecting to a feeling of safety that gives your inner-being the capacity to walk your healing journey.

6. **Return to the Light**

If you have practiced one, or more, of the optional steps then return to the light, finding peace in it. Return your focus to the light filling your orb and the rest that it gives you. This step helps the unconscious remember itself before returning to your immediate life. The path you take in must always be the path you take out.

7. Return to the Sacred Silence

8. Observe Senses

9. Give Thanks

Open Mind

Open Mind is a practice of Mental Alchemy from my personal practice, The Art of Self-Creation. It is a practice within which we apply Sacred Silence, mental poise, body control, and willpower to awaken our connection with Spirit. We apply spiritual poise and body control to awaken our pineal gland. Through this action we awaken our connection with Spirit and 'open' our mind.

When we 'open' our mind we strengthen our connection with Spirit. A person may apply this practice to open their mind in a way that allows them to experience Spirit in a more direct and profound way. Open Mind is a powerful practice that can deepen a person's connection with the spirit of their life.

It is wise, if seeking to practice Open Mind, that a person is conscious of how open their mind becomes. The experience of Spirit is powerful and is capable of creating madness. Be conscious of how open your mind is and apply Open Mind with wisdom.

Method

1. Enter Sacred Silence

Methods of body control and mental alchemy require Sacred Silence so that the unconscious has the space it needs to shift states. Without Sacred Silence, being the meditative state of mind, this practice is made much more difficult.

2. Turn your Awareness to your Energetic Connection with the World Around you

Awareness is very Powerful. When we turn our awareness to a part of our mind we empower that part of our mind. By turning our awareness to the part of our unconscious that holds our energetic connection with the world around us we strengthen our connection with Spirit. We turn our awareness to the processes of our pineal gland. A person may also turn their awareness to their spirit, the part of them that is their energetic formation, if they know where to find it to receive the same results.

3. Remain Poised in this Stance

Remain poised in the 'spirit stance' as best able. Maintain focus, remembering that Sacred Silence is the vehicle for the energetic movement. Holding the mind in this way is a 'spirit stance'. It is to hold our spirit, our energetic manifestation, in a certain way. Through this 'stance', and applying body control, we create shifts within our unconscious.

4. Return to Sacred Silence

When you are finished the practice return to Sacred Silence. Focus briefly on relaxation and the vision of Sacred Silence.

5. Observe Senses

6. Give Thanks

The Oneness Prayer

(An incantation is a series of words used for a spell or charm)

The Oneness Prayer helps us reconnect to our Self as an expression and extension of Nature.

The Oneness Prayer should be used when either laying flat on the ground or walking in nature.

The Oneness Prayer has been received by the spirit of Mother Earth and spirits of Nature. They have spoken that they will receive people through The Oneness Prayer. For those who seek closeness with the spirit of Mother Earth this is a great gift. Mother Earth and the spirits of Nature would be grateful to have others seek this closeness.

Method

1. **Enter the Sacred Silence as Best Able**

It is advised to enter the Sacred Silence before going into the prayer. Sacred Silence is the vehicle of spiritual movement so it helps you feel the prayer. Have patience with yourself.

2. Repeat the Following Incantation

My skin is bark
My bones are roots
My blood is sap
X3
I am the Earth
X3

This incantation is empowered energetically. The spirits of Nature and Mother Earth have taken in this incantation and will likely hear when it is spoken. The incantation, when spoken from the Sacred Silence, respected for its Power, and used with the other parts of this prayer can create a powerful shift within the unconscious. A person may see Nature in new ways or feel movement within their unconscious being.

3. Envision yourself as the Earth Walking

Envision your body made of soil. You are the earth walking. Feel that connection. It is Balance. You are an extension of Balance. Envision you body made of soil. Sacred Silence is the vehicle that allows this envisioning to connect you with the spirit of Earth.

4. Rest into The Vision and Prayer

Once having spoken the incantation and keeping the vision, do your best to let it be restful. Keep the Sacred Silence while envisioning your body as soil. Let it be a thing that connects you and helps you rest. If you are laying down this may mean relaxing into your earth. If you are walking this may mean feeling the nature around you in a peaceful way. You may even find that you see nature in a new way, as though a shroud has been removed from your eyes.

5. Stay in Prayer as Long as You Feel is Well

Stay in this prayer as long as you feel. Use it whenever you need. You can repeat the incantation as many times as you feel is well. It is a good way to keep the prayer if you feel like you need it.

6. **Give thanks to the Mother Earth and the spirits of Nature**

The Incantation is meant to help us reconnect with our Nature.

The first phrase is spoken three times. It reminds us that we are as trees who have lifted up their roots and started walking around. We are a part of Mother Earth. When we are as One in our life is also where we are as the trees in our Way.

The second phrase reinforces that we are as One with Mother Earth. We are all the earth. We are all as One. Where we are well in our Way is also where we are connected to our True Nature.

The Oneness Prayer is an easy to apply and useful prayer. It can be used at any time to help us reconnect to our Nature. When we pray this prayer consistently we grow closer to Nature, being also our own. We may find, as we continue with this prayer, that our will strengthens in finding health. It is Mother Earth taking us back to Herself. As we continue we will find a deeper connection to Nature to awaken within us. This is the connection that lives underneath our suffering and our distance. The Oneness Prayer is a powerful way to reconnect with our roots and return to our alignment with Mother Earth. It is an easy to apply prayer that we can use at any time to reclaim that connection.

When we pray this prayer we create movement within our unconscious being to return to our Balance, our Earth. We may find that as we continue using this prayer that we are brought into healing movements. A person may find that they are urged into releasing the suffering they carry through applying the prayer consistently. The prayer's energetic operation pushes against the suffering that keeps us away from our Balance, our Earth. The spirit of Mother Earth, through the prayer, pushes to realign our unconscious with who we are in alignment with Her spirit. Our connection with Mother Earth is our connection with Balance. Our Balance is kept in alignment with Mother Earth so to turn toward our connection with Her can be a powerful healing movement.

If the prayer raises intense emotions it is wise to take a moment at the end of the prayer to count your blessings or remember what you love about yourself. This helps to resolve the healing movement in a good way.

The Oneness Prayer is a pathway toward closeness with the spirit of Mother Earth. Mother Earth has a spirit of Her own. She is like a goddess. The Oneness Prayer is a pathway toward Her spirit for those who seek Her.

The Prayer of True Purity

In the first book of The Way of Unity, titled The Path of Fullness, there are thirteen Pillars. They are The Pillars of Unity. The Pillars are fundamental teachings of The Way of Unity. Each Pillar is an expression of a Universal Principle. With each Pillar there is a prayer offered to help people connect to and cultivate the Pillar's universal qualities within themself. This prayer is the prayer of the Pillar of True Purity. It is a prayer that helps us align with our Sacred Heart.

The essence of creation is Oneness. It is for this reason that to align with origin is the home of sustenance. That alignment is True Purity. Truth leads into sustenance, for all things are both Truth and Oneness manifesting. The Pillar of True Purity explains that the origin of life is the Purity of Life. If origin did not sustain itself, creation would implode. To align with our origin is our path to sustenance. To align with the nature of our origin is our True Nature. This is the essence of the Pillar of True Purity.

We all have a Sacred Heart. As our soul came into the world it left a piece of itself behind. That piece it left behind is our Sacred Heart. Our Sacred Heart is the part of our energetic being that is kept in the Oneness of creation. Within our Sacred Heart exists our alignment. To pray the prayer of True Purity is to seek to deepen your connection with your Sacred Heart. It is to ask that part of your being to help you return to your alignment.

The essence of creation is fluid. There is structure in that fluidity, however the structure does not attach to its Way. The tree does not hold to the wind as it passes, neither does the river cling to its bank. The fullness of our True Purity is detached into connection. It lets go into alignment with our Sacred Heart and through this it frees the True Nature within. We become as the tree who does not hold to the wind. We become as the river, made ceaseless in our Way. In the prayer of True Purity we let go, poised in our Sacred Heart and seeking alignment with our True Nature.

The Prayer of True Purity is a Healing Trance. The healing trance is a method of meditation/prayer that is unique to The Way of Unity. Within Sacred Silence we hold our spirit, our mind, in a shape that calls in healing. As the unconscious begins moving to align with the shape of the spirit, the mind, a trance state awakens, urging the unconscious into alignment with fullness. The healing trance is poising the mind and spirit in a shape that causes healing while within the Sacred Silence. The Prayer of True Purity is a healing trance.

In The Prayer of True Purity the words of the prayer are as an incantation. We speak them to 'call in' the Pillar's energetic qualities.

The first part of The Prayer of True Purity is The Unity Prayer. It is the essential prayer of The Way of Unity. The Unity Prayer is its own healing trance. To learn more about The Unity Prayer and The Way of Unity see: The Path of Fullness - Book 1 of The Way of Unity or visit WisdomandUnity.com

The Prayer of True Purity is a powerful meditation/prayer anyone may use to realign their unconscious with the fullness of their life. To apply the prayer of True Purity consistently is a powerful tool.

You do not need to speak the words of The Prayer of True Purity to practice the method and receive its medicine.

Words of The Prayer of True Purity:
Creator, Spirit-Who-Moves-In-All, Mother Earth

Make me as stone
Flowing like water
In the Truth of my soul
In my True Nature
And moving always unto Unity
And Their image in me

Help me stand like the trees
And sing my soul song in every step
Help me know my Sacred Heart
And in being be Pure as the Earth

Method

1. Enter the Sacred Silence

Sacred Silence is an important part of the healing trance. It is like the 'meditative' mind.

2. Poise your Spirit in Alignment with your Sacred Heart

Poise your spirit in alignment with the part of your heart that is as One with creation. Stand in your mind and spirit as though you are in alignment with your innermost nature.

3. Let Go while Remaining Poised on your Sacred Heart

After having poised your spirit in alignment with your Sacred Heart let go of everything else. Let go, even, of what appears as being close to your Sacred Heart. Completely let go into that poise. Correct your poise if required, that the spirit may remain aligned with the part of your heart that is as One with creation.

Remain poised in your connection without assumption and continuing to 'surrender'. Hold nothing. Let everything move, remaining in the connection you have found. Letting go wholly into alignment with your Sacred Heart creates a powerful trance state as the Sacred Heart is given the chance to realign the unconscious.

4. Remain in the Trance, Making Sure to Offer Space for Healing to Occur

Take rest in the prayer as best able while offering space for movement to occur within your unconscious. The prayer will become a healing trance state if the method has been followed. The healing trance will realign your unconscious with the fullness of your life. Stay as long as feels well

5. Return to Sacred Silence

Before returning to your immediate life, consciously return to the Sacred Silence. This 'completes the circle' of the practice.

6. Observe Senses

Once finished your prayer return to your immediate life. There may be powerful energies with you when you return. We are not meant to stay in these energies except to let them move as they will. Do not hold to them and do not push them away. It is not effortful, that we return to our immediate life. It is a gentle movement. It is much like the current of a river slowly returning to a calm place after a storm. Remember your immediate life. Observvе your five senses.

7. Give Thanks

In The Prayer of True Purity The Sacred Heart may test a person to see if they are ready to let go and step into Life. A person must let go into Life, releasing their attachments and judgements, their preconception, or they will not find the medicine of this prayer.

I want to emphasize that any and all people may use this prayer to deepen their connection with their own ways. This practice is not defined by a tradition. It is offered to help us remember the Spirit of our own ways. It is offered to strengthen those who seek their own Way, in any and every way of knowing. We are all messiah. Our Way in this world is exactly where we are messiah. The Sacred Heart and True Purity are universal. They are a way to reconnect to the part of us that is deeply integrated into our Way in this life. I ask that all people who use this prayer make it their own. It has never been mine.

This prayer may be used as a way to facilitate the healing journey. By using this prayer we may connect to the part of us that 'fills the space' after a healing movement. As we deepen our connection to our Sacred Heart we may find that our works of healing find a place beyond the suffering. This prayer is a Powerful way to fulfill the works of healing many are seeking to accomplish.

As one connects with their Sacred Heart, releasing their suffering, they may have their suffering raise to the surface of their mind. As the suffering is released a person may need to 'pass through' the difficult emotions. If this occurs make sure to resolve the healing cycle by remembering what you are grateful for and what you love about yourself. If this occurs it is your Sacred Heart helping you walk your healing journey. To align with the Sacred Heart is to overcome suffering.

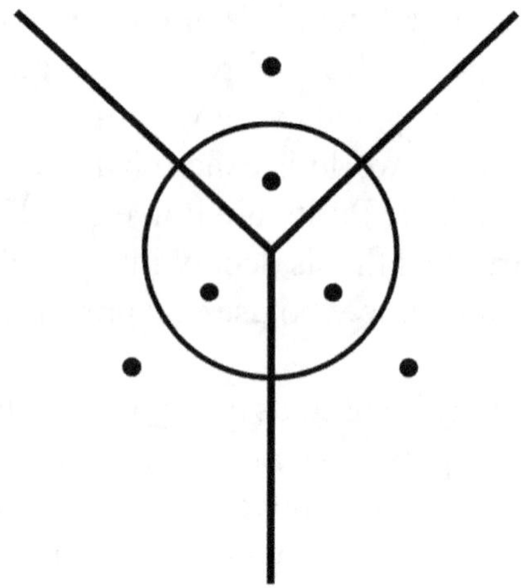

"All is One"

"I will throw the doors of The Temple wide, that all who seek may Know"

Too learn more about the author of this work and the work of the author see: **WisdomandUnity.com**

www.ingramcontent.com/pod-product-compliance
Lightning Source LLC
Chambersburg PA
CBHW050600070726
47689CB00050B/507

9781069282200